How to start working in IT starting from zero

James Relington

DEDICATION

This book is dedicated to all the professionals working tirelessly to secure digital systems and protect organizations from ever-evolving threats. To the cybersecurity teams, IT administrators, and identity management experts who ensure safe and seamless access for users—your work is invaluable. And to my family and friends, whose support and encouragement made this journey possible, thank you.

AKNOWLEDGEMENTS

I would like to express my deepest gratitude to everyone who contributed to the creation of this book. To my colleagues and mentors in the cybersecurity field, your insights and expertise have been invaluable. To the organizations and professionals who shared their experiences and best practices, your contributions have enriched this work. A special thank you to my family and friends for their unwavering support and encouragement throughout this journey. Finally, to the readers, thank you for your interest in identity lifecycle management—may this book help you navigate the evolving landscape of digital security with confidence.

Understanding the IT Industry

The Information Technology (IT) industry is one of the most dynamic and rapidly evolving sectors in the world. It encompasses a vast range of careers, technologies, and opportunities that span across different fields such as software development, cybersecurity, networking, cloud computing, data science, and IT support. The industry is crucial to nearly every sector, from healthcare and finance to education and entertainment. Understanding how the IT industry functions, its key components, and what drives its continuous growth is essential for anyone looking to start a career in this field.

One of the defining characteristics of the IT industry is its constant evolution. New technologies, programming languages, and frameworks emerge regularly, requiring professionals to stay updated and continuously learn. Unlike many traditional industries, IT does not have a single career path. Instead, it offers multiple specializations, each with its own set of skills, tools, and certifications. For example, someone interested in building applications can focus on software development, while another person may find their passion in securing digital systems through cybersecurity. The flexibility of IT allows individuals to switch between roles or even combine skills from different areas to create a unique career path.

The backbone of the IT industry consists of hardware and software. Hardware includes physical devices such as computers, servers, routers, and mobile devices that enable computing and connectivity. Software, on the other hand, includes operating systems, applications, databases, and cybersecurity tools that allow hardware to function efficiently. IT professionals often specialize in either hardware-related roles, such as network engineering and system administration, or software-related roles, such as programming and web development. However, many IT jobs require knowledge of both areas to troubleshoot issues and optimize systems.

One of the main drivers of the IT industry's growth is the increasing reliance on technology in daily life and business operations. Organizations of all sizes depend on IT for communication, data storage, automation, and security. The demand for IT professionals continues to rise as businesses invest in digital transformation, cloud computing, and artificial intelligence to remain competitive. This growth leads to a constant need for skilled individuals who can manage, develop, and secure IT infrastructure. As a result, IT careers tend to offer competitive salaries, job stability, and opportunities for advancement.

Understanding the IT industry also requires recognizing the different employment models available. Many IT professionals work full-time for companies, providing ongoing support, development, or security services. Others work as freelancers or consultants, offering specialized expertise to multiple clients. The rise of remote work has also expanded opportunities for IT professionals to work from anywhere in the world. Some people choose to work in startups, where they can contribute to innovative projects in a fast-paced environment, while others prefer large corporations with structured career progression and enterprise-level projects. The variety of work environments in IT allows individuals to find roles that match their preferences and lifestyles.

Another important aspect of the IT industry is the emphasis on problem-solving and innovation. IT professionals are often tasked with identifying and resolving technical issues, improving system performance, and developing new solutions to meet business needs. Whether it is debugging a piece of code, designing a network infrastructure, or implementing cybersecurity measures, IT professionals must think critically and creatively. The ability to troubleshoot and adapt to new challenges is a fundamental skill in this industry, and those who excel in problem-solving tend to advance quickly in their careers.

Education and training in IT are highly diverse, with multiple paths leading to a successful career. Some people pursue formal degrees in computer science, information technology, or related fields. Others take alternative routes, such as self-study, coding bootcamps, online courses, or certifications. Many IT professionals start without a traditional degree and instead build their skills through hands-on experience, projects, and industry-recognized certifications. The accessibility of IT education makes it possible for individuals to enter the industry regardless of their background, as long as they are willing to learn and practice consistently.

Certifications play a significant role in IT careers, particularly for those who do not have formal degrees. Many organizations recognize certifications as proof of expertise in specific areas such as networking, security, cloud computing, and project management. Popular certifications include CompTIA A+, Network+, and Security+, Cisco's CCNA, AWS certifications for cloud computing, and Microsoft certifications for various IT roles. Earning certifications not only helps individuals validate their skills but also increases their employability and salary potential.

The IT industry is also known for its strong community and collaborative culture. Many professionals engage in online forums, open-source projects, and local meetups to share knowledge and learn from others. Platforms such as GitHub, Stack Overflow, and LinkedIn provide opportunities to connect with experienced professionals, contribute to projects, and gain insights into industry trends. Participating in these communities helps newcomers gain exposure, receive mentorship, and stay updated on the latest developments in technology.

Despite the many advantages of working in IT, it is important to acknowledge some of the challenges. The rapid pace of technological advancements means that professionals must continuously update their skills to remain relevant. The industry can be highly competitive, especially in specialized roles, requiring individuals to stand out through experience, certifications, and problem-solving abilities. Some IT jobs also involve working long hours, troubleshooting urgent technical issues, or handling high-pressure situations, particularly in cybersecurity, system administration, and IT support roles. However, for those who enjoy learning and adapting to new challenges, IT provides a rewarding and fulfilling career.

The future of the IT industry looks promising, with emerging technologies such as artificial intelligence, blockchain, and quantum computing shaping the next generation of digital solutions. Businesses are increasingly investing in automation, cybersecurity, and cloud infrastructure, creating new job opportunities and career paths. As industries become more reliant on data and digital systems, IT professionals will play a crucial role in ensuring efficiency, security, and innovation. The continuous growth of the industry makes it an attractive field for those looking to build long-term careers with endless possibilities.

For individuals starting from zero, the key to entering the IT industry is curiosity, persistence, and a willingness to learn. With a vast array of resources available, anyone can develop the skills needed to secure an entry-level IT job and grow within the field. Whether through formal education, self-study, or hands-on projects, the opportunities to enter and advance in IT are more accessible than ever. By understanding the industry's structure, job roles, and learning paths, beginners can take their first steps toward a successful and rewarding career in IT.

Choosing the Right IT Career Path

Choosing the right career path in the IT industry is a crucial decision that can shape your professional future. With so many specializations available, it can be overwhelming to determine which field aligns best with your interests, skills, and career goals. The IT industry is vast and diverse, offering opportunities in software development, cybersecurity, networking, cloud computing, data science, IT support, and many other areas. Understanding the different career paths and how they fit your personal strengths and aspirations is essential to making an informed decision.

One of the first steps in choosing an IT career path is assessing your interests and strengths. Some people are naturally inclined towards problem-solving and logical thinking, making them well-suited for roles in programming, system administration, or cybersecurity. Others enjoy working with hardware and physical infrastructure, which may lead them towards networking or IT support. Those with a passion for creativity and design might find web development, UI/UX design, or game development appealing. Identifying what excites you and aligns with your skills is a fundamental step in narrowing down your options.

Another important factor to consider is the level of technical expertise required for different roles. Some IT careers demand strong programming skills, such as software development and data science, where knowledge of languages like Python, Java, or JavaScript is essential. Other careers, such as IT support and system administration, may focus more on troubleshooting, hardware, and system configurations rather than coding. Cybersecurity, a highly specialized field, requires an understanding of networks, encryption, ethical hacking, and risk management. Cloud computing and DevOps involve automation, infrastructure management, and cloud-based technologies that optimize business operations. The technical demands of each career path vary, so it is important to choose a path that matches your willingness to learn and develop specific skills.

Understanding job market demand and career growth potential is also a key consideration. Some IT roles, such as cybersecurity specialists, cloud engineers, and data scientists, are in high demand and offer excellent job security and salaries. As businesses continue to adopt cloud technologies and digital security measures, professionals in these areas are highly sought after. On the other hand, traditional IT roles like technical support and help desk positions may have more competition and lower salaries but can serve as stepping stones to more advanced careers. Researching job trends, salary expectations, and future demand can help you make an informed choice about which path to pursue.

Another critical aspect of selecting the right IT career is considering how much education and certification are required for each field. Some IT careers, such as software development and web development, allow individuals to enter the industry with self-taught skills and a strong portfolio. Others, like cybersecurity and cloud engineering, often require industry-recognized certifications such as CompTIA Security+, Cisco Certified CyberOps Associate, AWS Certified Solutions Architect, or Microsoft Azure certifications. Networking professionals may need to obtain Cisco's CCNA or CompTIA Network+ certifications, while those interested in database management and business intelligence might benefit from SQL and data analytics certifications. Knowing which credentials are valuable in your chosen field can guide your learning path and help you become job-ready faster.

Gaining hands-on experience is an important part of deciding on a career path. Many people start experimenting with different IT disciplines before committing to a specific area. Setting up a home lab, working on personal coding projects, contributing to open-source software, or volunteering for IT-related tasks can provide insight into what you enjoy and excel at. Online platforms offer free and paid resources to explore different IT careers, including interactive coding exercises, cybersecurity challenges, cloud computing labs, and virtual networking simulations. Taking the time to explore various fields can help you make a more confident decision about which career suits you best.

Networking with professionals in the IT industry can also provide valuable insights into different career paths. Connecting with people who work in various IT roles through LinkedIn, online forums, or local meetups can give you a realistic view of what different jobs entail. Engaging with IT professionals allows you to ask questions about their daily responsibilities, challenges, and career growth opportunities. Many experienced IT workers are willing to share advice and mentorship with newcomers, helping them navigate their career choices more effectively.

Work-life balance and job flexibility are additional factors to consider when choosing an IT career. Some IT roles, such as system administration, cybersecurity, and IT support, may require working on-call shifts, responding to emergencies, or handling system failures outside of regular hours. Other careers, such as software development and cloud engineering, offer more remote work opportunities and flexible schedules. Understanding the work environment and potential job demands of each career path can help you choose a field that aligns with your lifestyle and personal preferences.

Your long-term career goals should also play a role in your decision. Some IT professionals prefer technical roles and enjoy mastering specific technologies, while others may aspire to move into management positions, such as IT project management, technical leadership, or chief information officer (CIO) roles. Certain IT careers offer more opportunities for leadership and strategic decision-making, while others focus primarily on hands-on technical expertise. If you have an interest in leading teams or managing projects, gaining experience in IT project management methodologies, such as Agile or Scrum, may be beneficial.

The IT industry is also highly adaptable, allowing individuals to transition between different career paths over time. Many professionals start in entry-level IT support roles before moving into cybersecurity, networking, or cloud computing. Others begin as software developers and later transition into DevOps, data science, or AI-related fields. The ability to shift between careers within IT is one of the industry's greatest advantages, as new technologies and specializations continue to emerge. Keeping an open mind and being willing to learn new skills can open doors to new career opportunities, even if your initial choice evolves over time.

Choosing the right IT career path is a journey that requires self-exploration, research, and practical experience. It is important to take your time, experiment with different areas, and seek guidance from experienced professionals. The IT industry offers a wealth of opportunities, and finding the right path depends on your interests, skills, and long-term goals. Regardless of where you start, continuous learning and adaptability will be essential for success in the field. By making an informed decision and staying committed to growth, you can build a rewarding career in IT that aligns with your aspirations and strengths.

Essential IT Skills for Beginners

Entering the IT industry requires a combination of foundational technical knowledge and problem-solving abilities. The field is vast, with multiple career paths ranging from networking and cybersecurity to programming and system administration. While each specialization has its own set of required skills, there are certain essential skills that all IT professionals should possess. These core skills help beginners establish a strong foundation and make them more adaptable to different roles within the industry. Developing these skills early on can significantly improve career prospects and prepare individuals for the dynamic nature of IT work.

A fundamental skill for anyone starting in IT is understanding how computer systems work. This includes knowledge of computer hardware, software, and operating systems. Beginners should familiarize themselves with components such as CPUs, RAM, storage devices, and motherboards, as well as how these components interact to perform computing tasks. Understanding how different operating systems, such as Windows, Linux, and macOS, function is equally important. Knowing how to navigate these systems, configure basic settings, install software, and troubleshoot common issues provides a strong starting point for any IT career. Linux, in particular, is widely used in the industry, especially for servers and cloud environments, making it a valuable skill to learn.

Another critical skill for beginners is networking knowledge. Computer networks form the backbone of modern IT infrastructure, enabling communication between devices and systems. Learning about IP addresses, subnetting, DNS, and network protocols such as TCP/IP is essential for anyone interested in IT support, cybersecurity, or system administration. Understanding how data travels across networks and how different networking devices like routers, switches, and firewalls function allows beginners to diagnose and resolve connectivity issues. Gaining hands-on experience with network configuration and troubleshooting can be beneficial, as networking concepts apply to various IT roles.

Basic programming and scripting skills are also highly valuable, even for those who do not plan to become software developers. Learning a programming language such as Python, JavaScript, or Bash scripting can help automate repetitive tasks, streamline workflows, and improve efficiency in IT operations. Python, in particular, is widely used for automation, data analysis, and cybersecurity tasks. Writing simple scripts to manipulate files, process data, or automate system administration tasks can make IT professionals more efficient and capable of handling complex challenges. Even a basic understanding of programming logic and syntax can be an advantage in many IT careers.

Cybersecurity awareness is another essential skill for beginners. With the increasing number of cyber threats, IT professionals need to understand how to protect systems and data from attacks. Basic knowledge of encryption, authentication, firewalls, and antivirus software is crucial. Recognizing phishing attempts, securing passwords, and implementing best practices for data protection can prevent security breaches. Beginners should also learn about common vulnerabilities, such as malware, social engineering attacks, and network security risks, to ensure that they follow secure practices in their work environment. A strong foundation in cybersecurity principles is valuable regardless of the specific IT career path chosen.

Familiarity with databases and data management is another important skill. Many IT roles require working with data, whether it is for managing user information, analyzing system logs, or storing application data. Learning how databases function, understanding SQL queries, and working with database management systems such as MySQL or PostgreSQL can be beneficial. SQL is one of the most widely used languages for interacting with databases, and knowing how to retrieve, update, and manipulate data is a valuable skill. Even for those not pursuing a career in data science or database administration, the ability to handle data efficiently is a useful asset in IT.

Cloud computing is rapidly becoming a standard in IT, making cloud-related skills increasingly important. Many businesses are migrating to cloud-based solutions such as Amazon Web Services (AWS), Microsoft Azure, and Google Cloud Platform (GCP). Understanding cloud computing concepts, such as virtualization, storage, and cloud security, can open up numerous career opportunities. Learning how to deploy and manage applications in cloud environments, work with cloud storage, and configure virtual machines are valuable skills that can enhance an IT professional's ability to support modern infrastructure. Cloud platforms provide free-tier options that allow beginners to practice and develop hands-on experience.

Another key skill for beginners is troubleshooting and problem-solving. IT professionals frequently encounter technical issues that require logical thinking and diagnostic skills to resolve. Being able to identify the root cause of a problem, test different solutions, and apply fixes efficiently is a fundamental part of IT work. Troubleshooting requires patience, analytical thinking, and an understanding of how different systems interact. Beginners should practice identifying common issues, researching solutions, and testing their problem-solving abilities through hands-on experience. Strong troubleshooting skills make IT professionals more effective and valuable in any technical role.

Effective communication skills are often overlooked but are crucial for success in IT. Many IT roles require explaining technical concepts to non-technical users, documenting processes, and collaborating with teams. Being able to convey information clearly, whether through written documentation, presentations, or verbal explanations, helps IT professionals work more efficiently and ensures that users understand how to resolve technical issues. Customer service skills are particularly important in IT support roles, where professionals must assist users with varying levels of technical knowledge. The ability to listen, ask the right questions, and provide clear instructions can make a significant difference in user satisfaction and problem resolution.

Time management and organizational skills are also essential in IT. Many IT professionals juggle multiple tasks, such as troubleshooting issues, managing updates, and working on long-term projects. Prioritizing tasks, setting deadlines, and using productivity tools can help beginners stay organized and efficient. Familiarity with project management methodologies, such as Agile or Scrum, can also be beneficial, particularly for those interested in software development or IT project management. Being able to manage workloads effectively ensures that projects are completed on time and that issues are addressed promptly.

A continuous learning mindset is perhaps the most important skill for anyone entering the IT industry. Technology is constantly evolving, with new tools, frameworks, and best practices emerging regularly. Staying updated with industry trends, learning new skills, and obtaining relevant certifications are crucial for career growth. Engaging with online courses, attending workshops, participating in IT forums, and experimenting with new technologies can keep professionals competitive and knowledgeable in their field. The willingness to adapt, learn, and grow is what ultimately defines success in the IT industry.

Developing these essential IT skills provides a solid foundation for beginners, allowing them to explore different career paths and find the area that best suits their interests. Whether focusing on networking, cybersecurity, programming, or cloud computing, acquiring these fundamental skills makes the transition into IT smoother and more rewarding. The ability to combine technical expertise with problem-solving, communication, and continuous learning ensures that individuals can thrive in the ever-changing landscape of information technology.

Learning Basic Computer and Networking Concepts

Understanding the fundamentals of computers and networking is essential for anyone looking to start a career in IT. Computers and networks form the backbone of modern technology, enabling businesses, individuals, and governments to communicate, store data, and execute critical operations. Having a solid grasp of how computers function, their components, and how they connect to networks provides a strong foundation for various IT roles. Whether someone is interested in cybersecurity, programming, or technical support, knowing the basics of computing and networking will help them troubleshoot issues, improve system efficiency, and develop more advanced technical skills over time.

A computer consists of hardware and software components that work together to perform tasks. Hardware refers to the physical parts of a computer, such as the central processing unit (CPU), memory, storage devices, motherboard, and input/output peripherals. The CPU acts as the brain of the computer, processing instructions and managing operations. Memory, commonly known as RAM, temporarily stores data and programs that the computer is actively using. Storage devices, such as hard drives and solid-state drives, provide long-term data retention. The motherboard connects all components and facilitates communication between them, while peripherals like keyboards, mice, and monitors allow users to interact with the system. Understanding how these components function and interact is crucial for diagnosing hardware issues and making informed decisions about upgrading or repairing a computer.

Software, on the other hand, consists of the operating system and applications that allow users to perform tasks. The operating system (OS) is the core software that manages hardware resources and provides an interface for users. Common operating systems include Windows, macOS, and Linux. Each OS has its own features, but they all perform similar functions, such as managing files, running programs, and handling security settings. Beginners should familiarize themselves with different operating systems, learning how to navigate their interfaces, configure settings, and troubleshoot common issues. Linux is particularly important in the IT field, as it is widely used for servers, cybersecurity, and cloud computing.

Networking is another essential aspect of IT, as it enables computers to communicate with each other and share resources. A computer network is a system of connected devices that exchange data. Networks can be classified based on their size and purpose, such as local area networks (LANs), wide area networks (WANs), and wireless networks. A LAN connects devices within a small geographical area, such as an office or home, while a WAN spans larger distances, often connecting multiple locations. Wireless networks, which use Wi-Fi technology, allow devices to connect without physical cables. Understanding how these networks operate helps IT professionals diagnose connectivity issues and optimize network performance.

The foundation of networking relies on protocols, which are sets of rules that define how data is transmitted between devices. The most important networking protocol is the Transmission Control Protocol/Internet Protocol (TCP/IP), which governs how data is sent and received over the internet and local networks. TCP/IP consists of multiple layers, including the application layer, transport layer, network layer, and data link layer. Each layer has a specific role in ensuring that data is properly formatted, transmitted, and delivered to the correct destination. Beginners should study these layers to understand how network communication works and why different issues arise in network troubleshooting.

IP addresses are crucial for identifying devices on a network. Every device connected to a network has a unique IP address, which serves as its digital identifier. There are two types of IP addresses: IPv4 and IPv6. IPv4, the older version, consists of four sets of numbers separated by dots, such as 192.168.1.1. Due to the growing number of internet-connected devices, IPv6 was introduced to provide a larger pool of addresses. IPv6 addresses are longer and written in hexadecimal format. Understanding how IP addresses work, along with subnetting and DNS resolution, helps IT professionals configure and troubleshoot networks more effectively.

Networking hardware includes routers, switches, modems, and firewalls. A router connects multiple networks and directs data packets to their intended destinations. It plays a crucial role in home and business networks, managing internet traffic and ensuring devices can communicate efficiently. Switches operate within a network, connecting multiple devices and allowing them to share data. Modems serve as the interface between a local network and an internet service provider, converting digital data into signals that can be transmitted over telephone or cable lines. Firewalls provide security by filtering incoming and outgoing traffic, protecting networks from unauthorized access and cyber threats. Understanding the function of these devices is essential for anyone working in IT, as they are the building blocks of network infrastructure.

Wireless networking has become increasingly important, with Wi-Fi technology enabling devices to connect without physical cables. Wi-Fi networks use radio signals to transmit data between routers and devices, offering flexibility and convenience. However, wireless networks are also more vulnerable to security threats, such as unauthorized access and data interception. IT professionals must understand encryption protocols like WPA2 and WPA3, which help secure wireless connections by encrypting data transmissions. Configuring secure Wi-Fi settings, managing access points, and troubleshooting connectivity issues are valuable skills in both personal and professional IT environments.

Troubleshooting network issues is a fundamental skill for IT beginners. Common problems include slow internet speeds, connectivity drops, and misconfigured devices. Basic troubleshooting steps involve checking physical connections, restarting network equipment, verifying IP configurations, and using diagnostic tools such as ping and traceroute. These tools help identify network bottlenecks, latency issues, and unreachable destinations. Learning to diagnose and resolve network problems efficiently is essential for anyone pursuing a career in IT support, cybersecurity, or system administration.

Understanding the basics of computer and networking concepts provides a strong foundation for more advanced IT skills. Computers and networks form the backbone of modern digital systems, making it essential for IT professionals to understand how they function. By gaining hands-on experience with different operating systems, configuring network devices, and troubleshooting connectivity issues, beginners can build the confidence and expertise needed to succeed in the IT industry. Whether pursuing a career in networking, cybersecurity, or software development, a solid understanding of these fundamental concepts will open doors to various opportunities and help individuals adapt to the ever-evolving world of technology.

Introduction to Operating Systems (Windows, Linux, macOS)

An operating system is the backbone of any computing device, serving as the bridge between hardware and software. It manages resources, allows users to interact with the system, and provides a platform for applications to run efficiently. Without an operating system, computers would not be able to function in a practical or user-friendly manner. Three of the most widely used operating systems in the world are Windows, Linux, and macOS. Each of these operating systems has its own strengths, weaknesses, and areas of application. Understanding how they work, their differences, and their use cases is essential for anyone pursuing a career in IT.

Windows, developed by Microsoft, is the most widely used operating system in the world. It is popular in both personal and business environments due to its ease of use, compatibility with a vast range of software, and strong support for gaming and productivity applications. Windows features a graphical user interface (GUI) that makes it accessible to users of all skill levels. Over the years, Microsoft has continuously improved Windows, adding features such as enhanced security, cloud integration, and virtual desktops. Windows is also widely used in enterprise environments, where it supports Active Directory, a powerful tool for managing users and devices in large networks. IT professionals working with Windows should understand system administration tasks such as managing user accounts, configuring network settings, troubleshooting system issues, and handling software installations.

One of the main advantages of Windows is its broad software support. Most commercial applications are designed to run on Windows, including office suites, creative tools, and business software. Additionally, Windows is the preferred platform for gaming, offering support for DirectX and a vast library of games. However, Windows is often criticized for its security vulnerabilities, as it is a common target for malware and cyberattacks. Microsoft has implemented various security features such as Windows Defender, BitLocker encryption, and automatic updates to enhance protection, but users must remain vigilant against threats. Regular system updates, proper antivirus protection, and safe browsing practices are necessary to maintain security on a Windows system.

Linux, in contrast, is an open-source operating system that is highly customizable and widely used in servers, cybersecurity, cloud computing, and development environments. Unlike Windows, which is owned and controlled by Microsoft, Linux is maintained by a global community of developers. It comes in many different distributions, or "distros," each designed for specific use cases. Some of the most popular distributions include Ubuntu, Debian, Fedora, and CentOS. Linux is known for its stability, security, and flexibility, making it the preferred choice for web servers, cloud infrastructure, and embedded systems.

One of the defining features of Linux is its command-line interface (CLI), which allows users to execute powerful commands for system management, file handling, and automation. While Linux does have graphical user interfaces, many advanced users prefer the command line because it provides greater control and efficiency. Learning basic Linux commands such as navigating directories, managing files, modifying user permissions, and installing software is crucial for IT professionals. Linux is also widely used in cybersecurity, where tools such as Kali Linux provide ethical hackers and security analysts with the necessary tools to test and secure systems.

Security is one of the biggest strengths of Linux. Because of its open-source nature, vulnerabilities are quickly identified and patched by the community. Linux systems also follow a strict permission structure that prevents unauthorized users from making critical changes. Unlike Windows, Linux does not rely heavily on antivirus software because most malware is designed to target Windows systems. However, security best practices, such as regular software updates and firewall configuration, are still necessary. The ability to customize and optimize Linux for specific needs makes it an essential skill for IT professionals working in network administration, DevOps, and cloud computing.

macOS, developed by Apple, is known for its sleek design, reliability, and seamless integration with Apple's ecosystem. It is widely used by creative professionals in fields such as graphic design, video editing, and music production due to its high-performance hardware and software optimization. macOS is built on a Unix-based foundation, making it similar to Linux in terms of stability and security. It offers a user-friendly interface while also providing a powerful command-line tool called Terminal, which allows users to execute Unix-based commands. Many developers and IT professionals appreciate macOS for its ability to run both Unix-based applications and commercial software with ease.

One of the key advantages of macOS is its integration with Apple devices and services. Features like Handoff, AirDrop, and iCloud allow seamless connectivity between Macs, iPhones, iPads, and other Apple products. This level of synchronization is particularly beneficial for users who rely on Apple's ecosystem for work and personal use. macOS also includes built-in security features such as Gatekeeper, which prevents unverified applications from running, and FileVault, which provides full-disk encryption to protect user data. Regular software updates from Apple ensure that security vulnerabilities are patched promptly.

Despite its strengths, macOS has some limitations. It is a closed-source operating system, meaning users have less control over customization compared to Linux. Additionally, it is more expensive since Apple hardware is required to run macOS legally. Many enterprise environments rely more on Windows and Linux due to cost and compatibility considerations. However, for those working in creative industries or software development, macOS remains a highly attractive option. Developers, in particular, benefit from macOS's compatibility with Unix-based tools, Docker, and the ability to run virtual machines for testing different operating systems.

Each operating system has its unique strengths, and IT professionals often need to work with multiple operating systems depending on their job roles. Windows is dominant in business environments and is essential for IT support, system administration, and enterprise applications. Linux is critical for networking, cybersecurity, cloud computing, and server management, offering unmatched customization and security. macOS, while more niche in enterprise settings, is highly valued in creative industries and development environments.

Learning how to navigate and troubleshoot each of these operating systems is an important step in building a successful IT career. Becoming proficient in Windows allows professionals to manage user accounts, configure networks, and troubleshoot system errors efficiently. Mastering Linux provides valuable skills for working with servers, automating tasks, and enhancing security. Familiarity with macOS allows IT professionals to support creative professionals and leverage Unix-based tools for software development. Developing a working knowledge of all three systems provides flexibility and a competitive edge in the IT industry, ensuring that professionals can adapt to various technical environments and job requirements.

Mastering Internet and Cybersecurity Basics

The internet has become an essential part of modern life, connecting billions of people, businesses, and devices across the world. It enables communication, entertainment, online shopping, remote work, and countless other activities. While the internet offers incredible convenience and opportunities, it also comes with significant risks. Cybersecurity threats, including hacking, phishing, malware, and data breaches, are constantly evolving. Understanding how the internet works and how to protect digital assets is crucial for anyone interested in IT. Mastering the fundamentals of internet technology and cybersecurity helps individuals navigate the digital world safely and prepares them for careers in IT security, networking, or system administration.

The internet is a global network of interconnected computers that communicate using standard protocols. At its core, the internet relies on the Transmission Control Protocol/Internet Protocol (TCP/IP) suite to transmit data between devices. The TCP/IP model consists of multiple layers, each responsible for different aspects of communication. The application layer handles user interactions, the transport layer ensures reliable data delivery, the network layer manages addressing and routing, and the data link layer controls communication between devices on the same network. Understanding these layers is essential for diagnosing network issues and improving connectivity.

Every device connected to the internet has a unique identifier called an IP address. IPv4, the older version of IP addressing, uses a 32-bit numeric format, limiting the number of possible addresses. Due to the expansion of internet-connected devices, IPv6 was introduced, offering a much larger address space with a 128-bit structure. IP addresses enable devices to communicate with each other by sending data packets through routers and switches. The Domain Name System (DNS) plays a crucial role in translating human-readable domain names, such as google.com, into IP addresses that computers can understand. Understanding IP addressing, subnetting, and DNS resolution is essential for managing and securing networks.

Cybersecurity is the practice of protecting systems, networks, and data from cyber threats. The increasing number of cyberattacks has made cybersecurity a top priority for individuals, businesses, and governments. Attackers use various methods to exploit vulnerabilities, steal information, and disrupt services. One of the most common threats is malware, which includes viruses, worms, trojans, ransomware, and spyware. Malware can spread through infected email attachments, malicious websites, or unsecured software. Antivirus programs and endpoint protection solutions help detect and remove malware, but users must also practice safe browsing habits and avoid downloading files from unknown sources.

Phishing is another prevalent cybersecurity threat that targets users through deceptive emails, messages, or websites. Attackers impersonate legitimate entities to trick victims into providing sensitive information, such as passwords, credit card details, or personal data. Phishing attacks often use urgent language to create a sense of panic, pressuring users to take immediate action. Recognizing phishing attempts involves checking sender addresses, verifying website URLs, and avoiding clicking on suspicious links. Multi-factor authentication (MFA) adds an extra layer of security by requiring an additional verification step, such as a temporary code sent to a mobile device, making it harder for attackers to gain unauthorized access.

Passwords play a critical role in cybersecurity, but many people use weak or easily guessable passwords, making them vulnerable to attacks. Strong passwords should be long, complex, and unique for each account. Password managers help generate and store secure passwords without requiring users to remember multiple credentials. Brute-force attacks, where hackers attempt to guess passwords through repeated attempts, highlight the importance of using complex passwords and enabling account lockout features. Organizations often enforce password policies that require periodic password changes and prevent the reuse of old passwords.

Firewalls act as barriers between trusted and untrusted networks, filtering incoming and outgoing traffic to block malicious activity. Hardware firewalls are physical devices installed between a network and the internet, while software firewalls run on individual computers or servers. Configuring firewalls properly ensures that only legitimate traffic is allowed while unauthorized access attempts are blocked. Intrusion Detection Systems (IDS) and Intrusion Prevention Systems (IPS) provide additional layers of security by monitoring network activity for signs of malicious behavior and taking automated actions to prevent attacks.

Encryption is a fundamental cybersecurity measure that protects data from unauthorized access. Encryption converts data into an unreadable format that can only be deciphered using a decryption key. Secure websites use Hypertext Transfer Protocol Secure (HTTPS) to encrypt communication between web browsers and servers, preventing data interception. Virtual Private Networks (VPNs) encrypt internet traffic, allowing users to browse securely, especially when using public Wi-Fi networks. End-to-end encryption is used in messaging apps to ensure that only the sender and recipient can read messages, preventing third parties from accessing sensitive conversations.

Social engineering is a tactic used by attackers to manipulate individuals into revealing confidential information. Unlike technical cyberattacks, social engineering exploits human psychology through deception and persuasion. Attackers may impersonate IT support personnel, company executives, or law enforcement officials to gain trust and obtain access credentials. Training employees to recognize social engineering tactics, verifying identities before sharing sensitive information, and maintaining a security-aware mindset are crucial for preventing these types of attacks.

Software updates and patch management play a significant role in cybersecurity. Many cyberattacks exploit vulnerabilities in outdated software, allowing attackers to gain control of systems or steal data. Operating systems, applications, and firmware must be regularly updated to fix security flaws and improve overall protection. Organizations often implement automated patch management systems to ensure that all devices receive security updates promptly. Individuals should enable automatic updates on their personal devices and avoid using unsupported software versions that no longer receive security patches.

Data backups are essential for mitigating the impact of cyberattacks, hardware failures, or accidental data loss. Ransomware attacks, where hackers encrypt a victim's files and demand payment for decryption, highlight the importance of having recent backups. Backup strategies include full backups, incremental backups, and cloud-based backups. Storing backups in multiple locations, such as external drives and cloud services, provides redundancy and ensures that data can be recovered in the event of a cyber incident. Organizations implement backup policies to protect critical data and maintain business continuity in case of disasters.

Cybersecurity awareness training is essential for both IT professionals and regular users. Many security breaches occur due to human error, such as clicking on malicious links, using weak passwords, or falling victim to scams. Organizations conduct regular security awareness programs to educate employees about best practices, threat detection, and incident response procedures. Security policies, such as acceptable use policies and data protection guidelines, help enforce cybersecurity measures and reduce risks. Developing a security-conscious mindset enables individuals to protect their digital identities, safeguard personal and business data, and contribute to a safer online environment.

Understanding the fundamentals of the internet and cybersecurity provides the knowledge necessary to navigate the digital world safely and securely. Learning how networks operate, recognizing common cyber threats, and implementing security best practices help protect personal and organizational data. Cybersecurity is a constantly evolving field, requiring continuous learning and adaptation to new threats. Developing a strong foundation in internet technology and cybersecurity principles is essential for IT professionals and anyone who interacts with digital systems. By staying informed and proactive, individuals can reduce their exposure to cyber risks and contribute to a more secure online environment.

Introduction to Programming and Scripting Languages

Programming and scripting languages are the foundation of modern computing, enabling software development, automation, and problem-solving in IT. These languages allow humans to communicate with computers by writing instructions that the machine can understand and execute. Programming is essential for building applications, websites, and operating systems, while scripting is widely used for automating repetitive tasks, managing system configurations, and enhancing cybersecurity operations. Learning how to program is a crucial step for anyone interested in working in IT, as it provides the ability to create, modify, and optimize software solutions.

Programming languages are designed to develop applications, process data, and perform complex operations. They follow strict syntax rules, requiring programmers to write code in a structured and logical manner. High-level programming languages, such as Python, Java, and C++, are widely used due to their readability, efficiency, and vast support from developer communities. These languages provide a balance between usability and performance, making them suitable for developing desktop applications, web services, and embedded systems. Programming languages vary in complexity and use cases, with some being optimized for specific tasks such as scientific computing, artificial intelligence, or game development.

Scripting languages, on the other hand, are primarily used for automating tasks and managing system operations. Unlike traditional programming languages, which often require compilation before execution, scripts are interpreted at runtime. This allows for quick modifications and execution without the need for compiling the code into machine language. Scripting languages such as Bash, PowerShell, and JavaScript are widely used in system administration, web development, and automation processes. Bash scripting is commonly employed in Linux environments to automate administrative tasks, manage file systems, and execute scheduled operations. PowerShell, developed by Microsoft, provides similar automation capabilities for Windows environments, allowing system administrators to manage network settings, install software, and troubleshoot configurations through command-line scripting.

One of the most widely used programming languages is Python, known for its simplicity, versatility, and extensive libraries. Python is an excellent language for beginners due to its clear syntax, which closely resembles human-readable language. It is used in a wide range of applications, including web development, data analysis, artificial intelligence, and cybersecurity. Python's extensive library ecosystem allows developers to perform complex tasks with minimal code, making it an ideal choice for automation and scripting as well. Many

IT professionals use Python to automate workflows, extract and analyze data, and create custom tools for system management.

JavaScript is another important language, primarily used for web development. It enables interactive and dynamic content on websites, allowing developers to build user-friendly interfaces, animations, and real-time applications. JavaScript runs on web browsers, making it essential for front-end development, but it can also be used on the server-side with frameworks like Node.js. Understanding JavaScript is crucial for web developers, as it powers a significant portion of modern websites and applications. Many IT professionals working in cybersecurity and automation also leverage JavaScript for writing scripts that interact with web applications, analyze data, and enhance security protocols.

For enterprise applications and large-scale software development, Java remains a widely used programming language. Java is known for its stability, portability, and object-oriented programming model, making it a preferred choice for building enterprise systems, mobile applications, and cloud-based services. The Java Virtual Machine (JVM) allows Java programs to run on different operating systems without modification, making it a cross-platform solution for business applications. Java is commonly used in banking systems, e-commerce platforms, and large-scale software infrastructures where performance and reliability are critical. IT professionals who want to work in backend development, mobile app development, or cloud computing can benefit greatly from learning Java.

For low-level programming and performance-critical applications, C and C++ are essential languages. These languages provide direct access to memory and system hardware, making them ideal for developing operating systems, embedded systems, and high-performance applications. C is widely used in system programming and cybersecurity, where understanding how software interacts with hardware is crucial. C++ extends C with object-oriented programming capabilities, making it a powerful language for game development, real-time simulations, and complex software architectures. Mastering C and C++ requires a deeper understanding of memory management, data structures, and algorithm optimization, but these skills are highly valuable in the IT industry.

Another key scripting language is Shell scripting, which is commonly used in Unix and Linux environments. Shell scripts are powerful tools for automating tasks such as system monitoring, log management, and software deployment. System administrators rely on shell scripting to configure servers, automate backups, and manage network services. Bash, one of the most popular shell scripting languages, allows users to write scripts that execute multiple commands sequentially, reducing manual workload and improving efficiency. Mastering shell scripting is essential for IT professionals working in system administration, DevOps, and cloud computing.

PowerShell is a scripting language specifically designed for Windows system administration. It provides advanced automation capabilities, allowing IT professionals to manage user accounts, configure security settings, and monitor system performance through script-based commands. PowerShell integrates seamlessly with Windows Management Instrumentation (WMI) and Active Directory, making it a powerful tool for enterprise IT environments. IT professionals who work with Windows-based infrastructures should develop strong PowerShell skills to automate administrative tasks, improve security configurations, and optimize system performance.

For database management and data analysis, SQL (Structured Query Language) is a fundamental scripting language. SQL is used to query, manipulate, and manage relational databases, making it an essential skill for IT professionals working with data. SQL allows users to retrieve specific data, update records, and create reports, making it a critical tool for data analysts, database administrators, and software developers. Understanding SQL helps IT professionals work with large datasets, optimize database performance, and ensure data integrity in business applications.

Each programming and scripting language serves a different purpose, and IT professionals often learn multiple languages depending on their career goals. Beginners should start with languages that match their interests and job aspirations. Python is a great entry point for general programming and automation, while JavaScript is essential for web development. Java and C++ provide strong foundations for software engineering, while PowerShell and Bash scripting are crucial for system administration and IT operations. SQL is indispensable for database management and business intelligence. By mastering these languages, IT professionals gain the ability to develop software, automate tasks, manage networks, and enhance cybersecurity efforts.

Developing proficiency in programming and scripting languages is a key milestone in an IT career. Learning how to write clean, efficient, and well-documented code allows professionals to solve technical problems, create innovative solutions, and automate complex processes. Practicing coding regularly, working on personal projects, and participating in online coding challenges can help beginners improve their skills and gain confidence. As technology evolves, programming and scripting languages will continue to play a crucial role in IT, making them essential skills for anyone looking to build a successful career in the field.

Building Your First Simple Program

Creating a simple program is one of the most important steps in learning to code. Writing code and seeing it work in real time provides a sense of accomplishment and helps build confidence in programming skills. Many beginners start by learning the fundamentals of a programming language and then move on to writing their first basic program. This process involves understanding syntax, logic, and problem-solving techniques, which are essential for developing more complex applications in the future. The choice of programming language for the first program depends on the learner's interest and career goals, but Python is often recommended for beginners due to its simplicity and readability.

Before writing a program, it is important to set up the development environment. This typically includes installing a code editor or an integrated development environment (IDE) that supports the chosen language. For Python, popular choices include VS Code, PyCharm, and IDLE. JavaScript developers often use web-based environments such as CodePen or browser consoles, while those learning Java might opt for Eclipse or IntelliJ IDEA. Once the development environment is ready, the next step is writing a basic program that follows structured logic and executes a specific task.

One of the simplest programs a beginner can create is the traditional "Hello, World!" program. This program displays a simple message on the screen and helps the programmer understand how code execution works. In Python, the code for this program is straightforward:

```python
print("Hello, World!")
```

Running this script outputs the text "Hello, World!" to the console. Although simple, this program introduces the basic structure of a script, including function calls and output generation. Understanding how code is written, saved, and executed is the first step in programming. Modifying the message or experimenting with different outputs allows beginners to explore how the language handles text and variables.

Once the basic concept of printing output is understood, the next step is working with user input. Accepting input from users makes programs interactive and allows them to respond dynamically. In Python, input can be gathered using the input() function, which prompts the user to enter a value:

```python
name = input("Enter your name: ")

print("Hello, " + name + "!")
```

This program asks the user for their name and then displays a personalized greeting. It introduces the concept of variables, which store data entered by the user. Variables are fundamental in programming as they allow information to be stored, modified, and reused throughout a program. Understanding how variables work is crucial for building more advanced applications.

The next logical step in programming is performing simple arithmetic operations. A beginner-friendly example is a basic calculator that adds two numbers entered by the user. In Python, this can be done using:

```python
num1 = input("Enter first number: ")

num2 = input("Enter second number: ")
```

```
sum_result = float(num1) + float(num2)
```

print("The sum is: " + str(sum_result))

This program introduces the concept of data types, as numbers need to be converted from string format (which is how input() stores values) to numerical format (float) to perform mathematical operations. The final result is converted back to a string using str() so that it can be displayed. This simple calculator demonstrates how programming can be used to process and manipulate data dynamically.

With basic operations covered, control structures such as conditional statements can be introduced. These structures allow a program to make decisions based on user input or other conditions. A simple example is a program that checks if a number is even or odd:

```
num = int(input("Enter a number: "))
```

if num % 2 == 0:

```
    print("The number is even.")
```

else:

```
    print("The number is odd.")
```

This program introduces the if statement, which evaluates whether a condition is true or false. The modulus operator % is used to determine if a number is divisible by two, which helps classify it as even or odd. Control structures like if statements are essential for writing programs that respond intelligently to different inputs.

Loops are another fundamental concept in programming. They allow repetitive tasks to be automated, reducing the need for redundant code. A simple example of a loop is printing numbers from 1 to 10 using a for loop:

for i in range(1, 11):

```
    print(i)
```

This program demonstrates iteration, where a block of code runs multiple times. Loops are particularly useful for handling repetitive tasks, such as processing large datasets or performing calculations on multiple inputs. Understanding loops is necessary for building more complex programs that require repeated operations.

Functions provide another important aspect of programming, allowing code to be modular and reusable. A function is a block of code designed to perform a specific task and can be called multiple times within a program. A simple example of a function that calculates the square of a number is:

```
def square(num):

    return num * num

result = square(5)

print("The square of 5 is:", result)
```

This function takes an input value, processes it, and returns the result. Functions make programs more organized and easier to maintain, especially as projects grow in complexity. Writing functions also encourages code reuse, making development more efficient.

Once these basic concepts are understood, beginners can start experimenting with more creative programs, such as simple games or text-based applications. A classic example is a number-guessing game where the computer selects a random number, and the user attempts to guess it:

```
import random

secret_number = random.randint(1, 10)

guess = 0
```

```
while guess != secret_number:

    guess = int(input("Guess a number between 1 and 10: "))

    if guess < secret_number:

        print("Too low!")

    elif guess > secret_number:

        print("Too high!")

print("Congratulations! You guessed the correct number.")
```

This program introduces random number generation, loops, and user interaction. It keeps running until the user correctly guesses the number, demonstrating how programming logic can create engaging and interactive experiences.

Building a first program is an important milestone in learning to code. It provides a hands-on approach to understanding key concepts such as variables, input handling, control structures, loops, and functions. Practicing these basics allows beginners to develop problem-solving skills and gain confidence in writing more advanced programs. Experimenting with different ideas, modifying existing code, and gradually increasing program complexity are effective ways to improve programming abilities. With continuous practice, beginners can move beyond simple scripts and develop full-fledged applications that solve real-world problems.

Exploring IT Certifications and Their Importance

In the world of information technology, certifications play a crucial role in validating skills, demonstrating expertise, and enhancing career prospects. Unlike traditional degrees, which often require years of study, IT certifications offer a structured way to gain industry-recognized credentials in a shorter period. Many employers value certifications because they provide proof that a candidate has the necessary technical knowledge and practical skills to perform specific IT tasks. Whether someone is just starting in IT or looking to advance their career, earning relevant certifications can significantly increase job opportunities, salary potential, and professional credibility.

IT certifications are designed to assess an individual's proficiency in different areas of technology, including networking, cybersecurity, cloud computing, programming, and IT support. Some certifications focus on fundamental concepts, making them ideal for beginners, while others are designed for experienced professionals seeking to specialize in advanced topics. Certifications are often vendor-specific, meaning they are associated with a particular company's products and services, such as Microsoft, Cisco, Amazon Web Services (AWS), and Google Cloud. There are also vendor-neutral certifications that focus on general IT knowledge and best practices applicable across multiple platforms.

One of the most well-known entry-level certifications is the CompTIA A+, which is designed for individuals starting their IT careers. It covers fundamental topics such as hardware, operating systems, networking, security, and troubleshooting. The CompTIA A+ certification is widely recognized by employers and serves as a stepping stone for those interested in technical support, system administration, or help desk roles. Many professionals begin their IT journey with this certification before moving on to more specialized areas. It helps build a strong foundation in IT concepts, ensuring that candidates understand both the theoretical and practical aspects of computer systems.

For those interested in networking, the Cisco Certified Network Associate (CCNA) certification is one of the most respected credentials in the industry. It focuses on networking fundamentals, including IP addressing, routing, switching, and network security. The CCNA certification is ideal for individuals who want to pursue careers in network administration, network engineering, or IT infrastructure management. Networking professionals play a critical role in ensuring that organizations maintain reliable and secure connectivity, making this certification highly valuable in enterprise environments. Cisco certifications are structured in a way that allows individuals to advance from associate-level credentials to more advanced certifications such as the Cisco Certified Network Professional (CCNP) and the Cisco Certified Internetwork Expert (CCIE).

Cybersecurity is one of the fastest-growing fields in IT, and certifications in this area are in high demand. The CompTIA Security+ certification is an excellent starting point for individuals looking to enter the cybersecurity industry. It covers essential security concepts such as threat management, cryptography, identity management, and risk assessment. Security+ is often a requirement for entry-level cybersecurity jobs, as it provides a solid understanding of security fundamentals. For those looking to specialize further, certifications such as Certified Ethical Hacker (CEH), Certified Information Systems Security Professional (CISSP), and Offensive Security Certified Professional (OSCP) offer more advanced knowledge and hands-on experience in ethical hacking, penetration testing, and information security management.

Cloud computing has become a critical aspect of modern IT infrastructure, and cloud certifications can open doors to high-paying job opportunities. Amazon Web Services (AWS) offers several certifications, including the AWS Certified Solutions Architect, AWS Certified Developer, and AWS Certified SysOps Administrator. These certifications validate knowledge of cloud architecture, deployment, and management using AWS services. Microsoft Azure and Google Cloud also provide cloud certification programs that help professionals gain expertise in managing cloud environments. As more businesses move their operations to the cloud, certified cloud professionals are in high demand, making cloud certifications a valuable investment for IT careers.

For those interested in IT support and service management, the ITIL (Information Technology Infrastructure Library) certification is widely recognized. ITIL focuses on best practices for IT service management (ITSM), helping organizations improve efficiency, reduce downtime, and enhance customer satisfaction. ITIL certifications are beneficial for IT professionals working in help desk roles, IT operations, and project management. Understanding ITIL frameworks allows professionals to implement effective IT service strategies, making them valuable assets to businesses seeking to optimize their IT processes.

Software development and DevOps certifications are also highly beneficial for programmers and software engineers. Certifications such as the Microsoft Certified: Azure Developer Associate, Google Professional Cloud Developer, and Certified Kubernetes Administrator (CKA) validate skills in cloud-native application development and containerization. DevOps certifications, including the AWS Certified DevOps Engineer and the HashiCorp Certified Terraform Associate, focus on automation, continuous integration, and infrastructure as code (IaC). These certifications help developers and IT operations professionals collaborate more effectively in modern software development environments.

Earning IT certifications requires preparation, as certification exams are designed to test both theoretical knowledge and practical skills. Many certification providers offer study materials, training courses, and practice exams to help candidates prepare. Hands-on experience is also essential, as many certifications include performance-based questions that require candidates to demonstrate their ability to perform real-world IT tasks. Online labs, virtual environments, and sandbox simulations provide valuable opportunities for candidates to gain practical experience before attempting certification exams.

One of the advantages of IT certifications is their ability to help professionals stand out in a competitive job market. Employers often use certifications as a benchmark when hiring, as they provide a standardized way to evaluate a candidate's technical abilities. Certified professionals tend to have higher earning potential compared to non-certified individuals, as certifications validate specialized skills that are valuable to organizations. Many IT professionals report that earning certifications has led to career advancements, promotions, and opportunities to work on more challenging projects.

Maintaining certifications is an ongoing process, as technology continues to evolve. Many certifications require renewal through continuing education, recertification exams, or professional development activities. This ensures that certified professionals stay up to date with the latest industry trends and advancements. IT professionals should stay engaged in learning new technologies, earning additional certifications, and participating in training programs to remain competitive in the job market. Certifications are not just about passing an exam but about continuously improving skills and staying relevant in a rapidly changing field.

Certifications provide a clear and structured path for IT professionals to gain expertise, demonstrate competence, and advance their careers. Whether an individual is new to IT or an experienced professional seeking specialization, certifications offer valuable credentials that enhance employability and open doors to better job opportunities. Employers recognize the importance of certifications as a way to ensure that their IT staff possess the necessary skills to handle complex technology challenges. By earning relevant certifications, IT professionals can build a solid foundation for long-term success in the industry, staying competitive and adaptable as new technologies emerge.

Choosing Your First IT Certification

Selecting the right IT certification as a beginner is a critical decision that can shape the trajectory of a career in information technology. With so many certifications available, each focusing on different aspects of IT, it can be overwhelming to determine which one to pursue first. The choice should be based on career goals, personal interests, and the current level of technical knowledge. A well-chosen certification can open doors to entry-level job opportunities, validate foundational skills, and set a clear path for professional growth in specialized areas such as networking, cybersecurity, cloud computing, or IT support.

Before deciding on a certification, it is important to assess personal career goals and areas of interest within IT. Some individuals may be drawn to technical support roles, while others may want to specialize in networking, security, cloud computing, or software development. Understanding what excites and motivates an individual can help narrow down the options and prevent unnecessary time and effort spent on a certification that may not align with long-term career aspirations. Since IT is a broad field, having a clear direction from the beginning can make learning more efficient and enjoyable.

For those who are new to IT and looking to build a strong foundation, entry-level certifications such as the CompTIA A+ are an excellent starting point. The CompTIA A+ certification covers essential IT knowledge, including computer hardware, operating systems, troubleshooting, networking, and security. It is widely recognized by employers and is particularly valuable for individuals who want to work in IT support, help desk, or system administration. The certification consists of two exams, each testing different aspects of IT fundamentals. Earning the CompTIA A+ credential demonstrates a solid understanding of core IT concepts and provides a strong foundation for more advanced certifications in the future.

Networking is another essential area of IT that offers numerous career opportunities. For individuals interested in building and managing computer networks, the Cisco Certified Network Associate (CCNA) certification is a great choice. The CCNA covers networking fundamentals, IP connectivity, security concepts, and automation, making it an ideal certification for those looking to become network administrators, network engineers, or IT infrastructure specialists. Networking is a crucial component of IT infrastructure, and professionals with CCNA certification are highly valued in organizations that rely on strong network connectivity for their operations.

Cybersecurity is a rapidly growing field with increasing demand for skilled professionals. Beginners interested in cybersecurity may consider starting with the CompTIA Security+ certification. This certification provides a foundational understanding of security principles, including risk management, cryptography, network security, and threat detection. Security+ is often a requirement for entry-level cybersecurity roles such as security analysts, information security specialists, and SOC (Security Operations Center) analysts. Since cybersecurity threats continue to evolve, having a solid grasp of security fundamentals is essential for anyone looking to specialize in this area.

For individuals interested in cloud computing, certifications from major cloud service providers such as Amazon Web Services (AWS), Microsoft Azure, and Google Cloud can provide a strong foundation. The AWS Certified Cloud Practitioner certification is an entry-level credential that introduces cloud concepts, pricing models, security best practices, and AWS core services. Similarly, the Microsoft Certified: Azure Fundamentals certification is designed for those who want to learn about Microsoft's cloud platform. Cloud computing is transforming the IT industry, and having a cloud certification can significantly improve job prospects in cloud engineering, DevOps, and IT infrastructure roles.

Software development is another popular career path in IT, and certifications can help validate programming skills and knowledge of development frameworks. While many software developers rely on portfolios to showcase their coding abilities, certifications such as the Microsoft Certified: Azure Developer Associate, Google Associate Cloud Engineer, and Oracle Certified Java Programmer can provide additional credibility. These certifications demonstrate proficiency in software development, cloud-based applications, and programming languages, making them valuable for aspiring developers looking to break into the industry.

For individuals who are interested in IT service management, the ITIL (Information Technology Infrastructure Library) Foundation certification is a great starting point. ITIL focuses on best practices for managing IT services, improving efficiency, and aligning IT strategies with business objectives. This certification is beneficial for professionals working in IT support, IT operations, and project management, as it provides a structured approach to delivering high-quality IT services. ITIL-certified professionals are often sought after in enterprise environments where IT service management plays a crucial role in business success.

Once a certification is chosen, proper preparation is essential to passing the exam. Many certification providers offer study guides, training courses, and practice exams to help candidates build the necessary knowledge and confidence. Online learning platforms, community forums, and hands-on labs can also provide valuable resources for gaining practical experience. Practicing real-world scenarios, setting up virtual labs, and troubleshooting common IT issues can reinforce theoretical concepts and improve problem-solving skills.

Budget is another factor to consider when choosing a certification. Some certifications, such as the CompTIA A+ and CCNA, require multiple exams, which can increase the overall cost. Additionally, certification training courses and study materials may add to the expense. However, many free and low-cost resources are available online, including official documentation, video tutorials, and community-driven forums. Some employers may also offer reimbursement for certification exams as part of their professional development programs. Researching the cost of certification exams and available study resources can help candidates plan their certification journey more effectively.

Certifications are not just about passing an exam but also about developing real-world skills. While earning a certification can enhance a resume, employers also value hands-on experience and practical problem-solving abilities. Combining certification training with real-world projects, internships, or home labs can provide a well-rounded skill set that prepares candidates for the challenges of IT jobs. Certifications should be viewed as a stepping stone to building expertise and gaining credibility in the field.

After obtaining a first certification, the next step is leveraging it to secure job opportunities. Including the certification on a resume, LinkedIn profile, and job applications can help attract the attention of recruiters and hiring managers. Networking with professionals in the IT industry, joining online communities, and participating in job fairs can also increase visibility and open doors to potential job offers. Certifications demonstrate commitment to learning and professional growth, which can make a candidate stand out in a competitive job market.

Choosing the right IT certification is a crucial step in launching a successful career in technology. The decision should be based on career interests, job market demand, and long-term professional goals. Whether pursuing a career in IT support, networking, cybersecurity, cloud computing, or software development, earning an industry-recognized certification can provide a strong foundation for growth and advancement. With proper preparation, hands-on practice, and continuous learning, individuals can use certifications to build a rewarding and successful career in IT.

Self-Study vs. Formal Education in IT

One of the most important decisions aspiring IT professionals must make is whether to pursue self-study or formal education. Both paths offer unique advantages and challenges, and the choice largely depends on individual learning styles, career goals, and available resources. The IT industry is known for being accessible to those who are willing to learn independently, but formal education provides structured guidance and recognized credentials. Understanding the differences between these two approaches can help individuals make informed decisions about their education and career development in the technology field.

Self-study in IT is an attractive option for many because of its flexibility and cost-effectiveness. The internet provides an abundance of free and paid resources, including online courses, video tutorials, documentation, and community-driven forums. Many aspiring IT professionals start their journey by using platforms such as Coursera, Udemy, LinkedIn Learning, and freeCodeCamp to learn programming, networking, cybersecurity, and other technical skills. These platforms offer courses that cover foundational and advanced topics, allowing learners to progress at their own pace without the constraints of a formal classroom environment.

One of the biggest advantages of self-study is the ability to focus on specific areas of interest. IT is a vast field with many specializations, and self-learners can tailor their education to match their career goals. For example, someone interested in cybersecurity can take ethical hacking courses, study penetration testing techniques, and practice using security tools in virtual labs. Likewise, individuals who want to become software developers can learn programming languages such as Python, JavaScript, or Java through online tutorials and coding exercises. Self-study allows learners to skip irrelevant topics and dive directly into subjects that align with their desired career path.

Another benefit of self-study is hands-on learning. IT professionals are often expected to solve real-world technical problems, and self-learners can gain practical experience by setting up home labs, working on projects, and experimenting with different technologies. For networking enthusiasts, creating a virtual lab using tools like Cisco Packet Tracer or GNS3 can provide valuable hands-on experience. Cybersecurity learners can use penetration testing environments such as Hack The Box and TryHackMe to practice ethical hacking skills in a controlled setting. By applying knowledge in real-world scenarios, self-learners can develop problem-solving skills that are highly valued by employers.

Despite its advantages, self-study comes with challenges. One of the biggest obstacles is the lack of structure and guidance. Without a curriculum or instructor, self-learners must create their own learning plans, which can be overwhelming for beginners. It is easy to get lost in the vast amount of available information, leading to frustration and burnout. Additionally, self-study requires a high level of discipline and motivation. Unlike traditional education, where deadlines and assignments enforce accountability, self-learners must stay committed to their studies without external pressure. Those who struggle with time management or staying focused may find it difficult to progress consistently.

Formal education in IT provides a structured and comprehensive approach to learning. Colleges and universities offer degree programs in computer science, information technology, cybersecurity, and related fields. These programs follow a predefined curriculum that ensures students gain a well-rounded education covering theoretical concepts, programming, networking, databases, and system administration. Professors and instructors provide guidance, answer questions, and clarify complex topics, making it easier for students to grasp challenging subjects. The structured nature of formal education helps students develop a strong foundation before moving on to more advanced topics.

One major advantage of formal education is the recognition and credibility that comes with earning a degree. Many employers, particularly large corporations and government agencies, require candidates to have a bachelor's degree in a relevant field. Degrees demonstrate a level of commitment, discipline, and knowledge that employers value. Additionally, having a formal education can open doors to internship opportunities, career fairs, and networking events that help students connect with industry professionals and potential employers. These connections can be crucial for securing job opportunities and gaining practical experience before entering the workforce.

Another benefit of formal education is access to academic resources and support systems. Universities often provide students with access to research papers, libraries, software licenses, and computing facilities that may not be available to self-learners. Many institutions also offer tutoring services, mentorship programs, and career counseling to help students succeed academically and professionally. Collaboration with peers and participation in group projects can also enhance learning by exposing students to different perspectives and problem-solving approaches.

However, formal education has its drawbacks. One of the most significant disadvantages is the cost. Tuition fees for degree programs can be expensive, and not everyone can afford to invest in a four-year education. Student loans can create financial burdens that take years to repay, making formal education a less attractive option for those seeking a quicker and more affordable entry into the IT field. In contrast, self-study and certification-based learning are often much more affordable, allowing individuals to gain skills without incurring significant debt.

Another limitation of formal education is its slower pace and lack of industry relevance in some cases. The IT industry evolves rapidly, and university curricula may not always keep up with the latest technologies, programming languages, or industry trends. By the time students graduate, some of the knowledge they acquired may already be outdated. In contrast, self-learners can quickly adapt to new developments and learn the latest tools and frameworks used in the industry. Many employers now prioritize practical skills and real-world experience over traditional degrees, making alternative learning paths more viable.

For those who want the best of both worlds, a hybrid approach combining self-study with formal education can be highly effective. Many university students supplement their studies with online courses, certifications, and personal projects to gain additional skills that may not be covered in their degree programs. Similarly, self-learners who want to validate their knowledge can pursue industry-recognized certifications such as CompTIA A+, CCNA, AWS Certified Cloud Practitioner, or Security+ to enhance their resumes. Combining academic education with hands-on experience and industry certifications creates a well-rounded skill set that increases employability and career opportunities.

Ultimately, the choice between self-study and formal education depends on individual goals, financial situation, and learning preferences. Self-study provides flexibility, affordability, and direct access to industry-relevant skills, making it ideal for those who prefer independent learning. Formal education offers structure, credibility, and networking opportunities, making it beneficial for those who seek a traditional academic experience and long-term career stability. Regardless of the chosen path, continuous learning and practical experience are essential for success in the IT industry. The most important factor is staying committed to acquiring knowledge, building skills, and applying them in real-world situations to grow as an IT professional.

Free and Paid Resources for Learning IT Skills

Learning IT skills has never been more accessible, thanks to the vast number of free and paid resources available online. Whether someone is a complete beginner or an experienced professional looking to expand their knowledge, there are numerous platforms, courses, and tools designed to help individuals gain expertise in networking, cybersecurity, programming, cloud computing, and other IT fields.

With so many options, it is important to understand the advantages of both free and paid learning resources to make informed decisions about which approach works best for different learning styles and career goals.

Free resources provide an excellent starting point for those who want to explore IT without making a financial commitment. Many well-established platforms offer high-quality content at no cost, making it possible to gain foundational knowledge before deciding to invest in paid courses or certifications. Websites such as freeCodeCamp, Codecademy, and Khan Academy provide interactive tutorials on programming, web development, and computer science principles. These platforms are designed for beginners and provide step-by-step guidance to help learners build coding skills through hands-on exercises. Free resources allow individuals to experiment with different topics and find out which area of IT interests them the most before committing to a more structured learning path.

Massive Open Online Courses (MOOCs) are another valuable source of free IT education. Platforms like Coursera, edX, and Udacity offer free access to high-quality university-level courses taught by professors from institutions such as Harvard, MIT, and Stanford. While these courses often provide an option to earn a paid certificate, the core content, including video lectures, assignments, and quizzes, is typically available for free. MOOCs cover a wide range of IT topics, including cybersecurity, cloud computing, machine learning, and ethical hacking. They provide an excellent way to gain theoretical knowledge from reputable sources while allowing learners to study at their own pace.

YouTube is one of the most popular and widely used free resources for learning IT skills. Many experienced professionals and educators share in-depth tutorials, coding lessons, and troubleshooting guides on their channels. Channels like Traversy Media, NetworkChuck, The Net Ninja, and Tech With Tim provide high-quality content covering web development, networking, Linux administration, and cloud computing. Since YouTube is a video-based platform, it is particularly useful for visual learners who benefit from seeing step-by-step demonstrations of technical concepts. The availability of free tutorials from multiple instructors also allows learners to explore different teaching styles and find explanations that best suit their understanding.

Community forums and documentation sites are essential free resources for IT learners. Platforms such as Stack Overflow, GitHub, and Reddit host active communities where beginners and experts exchange knowledge, share solutions, and collaborate on projects. Stack Overflow is particularly useful for troubleshooting programming and technical issues, as it contains a vast database of questions and answers from professionals in various IT fields. GitHub provides access to open-source projects, allowing learners to study real-world code, contribute to repositories, and collaborate with experienced developers. Official documentation sites for programming languages, frameworks, and operating systems, such as Python.org, MDN Web Docs, and Microsoft Learn, offer authoritative and up-to-date information that helps learners develop strong technical skills.

While free resources provide an excellent foundation, paid resources offer additional benefits such as structured learning paths, instructor support, and industry-recognized certifications. Paid courses often include well-organized curriculums designed to take learners from beginner to advanced levels in a logical progression. Platforms such as Udemy, Pluralsight, and LinkedIn Learning offer affordable courses on a wide range of IT topics, including programming, cybersecurity, cloud computing, and IT project management. Many of these courses are created by industry professionals and include hands-on labs, quizzes, and projects to reinforce learning. The ability to receive direct support from instructors and participate in discussion forums can enhance the learning experience and provide answers to complex questions.

Subscription-based learning platforms such as Pluralsight, Cloud Academy, and A Cloud Guru specialize in IT and cloud-related training. These platforms provide structured courses tailored to specific certifications, including AWS, Microsoft Azure, Google Cloud, CompTIA, Cisco, and cybersecurity certifications. The advantage of subscription-based learning is that users gain unlimited access to a vast library of courses, practice exams, and hands-on labs for a fixed monthly or annual fee. This model is particularly beneficial for individuals preparing for IT certification exams, as it allows them to focus on multiple courses and learning paths within a single subscription.

Bootcamps and live training courses offer an immersive learning experience for those looking to fast-track their IT education. Coding bootcamps such as Le Wagon, General Assembly, and Flatiron School provide intensive training programs that focus on web development, data science, and cybersecurity. These programs typically last a few months and include live instruction, mentorship, and career support. While bootcamps can be expensive, they often offer job placement assistance and networking opportunities that help graduates secure employment in IT roles. For individuals who prefer a structured and guided learning environment, bootcamps provide a highly effective way to gain industry-ready skills in a short period.

Certification training programs are another category of paid resources that provide targeted preparation for IT exams. Organizations such as CompTIA, Cisco, Microsoft, AWS, and Google offer official training courses designed to help candidates pass certification exams. These programs often include hands-on labs, official study guides, and practice tests that simulate real exam conditions. Investing in official training materials can increase the chances of passing certification exams on the first attempt, saving time and effort in the long run. Many IT professionals view certification training as a worthwhile investment because certifications enhance job opportunities and salary potential.

Another advantage of paid resources is access to hands-on virtual labs and simulated environments. Platforms such as Cyber Range, TryHackMe, and Hack The Box provide interactive cybersecurity training, allowing learners to practice ethical hacking, penetration testing, and defensive security techniques in a safe environment. Similarly, cloud computing platforms like AWS, Azure, and Google Cloud offer free-tier access to cloud services, allowing users to build and experiment with cloud infrastructure at little or no cost. Hands-on experience is a crucial component of IT learning, and these paid resources provide an opportunity to gain real-world skills through practical application.

Choosing between free and paid resources depends on individual learning preferences, career goals, and financial considerations. Free resources are excellent for self-paced learners who are disciplined and motivated to explore IT topics independently. They provide an accessible entry point into IT without financial risk and allow learners to experiment with different subjects before committing to a paid course. Paid resources, on the other hand, offer structured learning, expert guidance, and additional support, making them ideal for individuals who prefer a more organized approach to education. The combination of free and paid learning materials can create a well-rounded learning experience, allowing individuals to build strong IT skills and advance their careers effectively.

Creating a Study Plan for IT Learning

Developing a structured study plan is essential for anyone looking to learn IT skills effectively. The field of information technology is vast, covering areas such as networking, cybersecurity, programming, cloud computing, and database management. Without a clear roadmap, it can be overwhelming to decide where to start and how to progress. A well-designed study plan helps learners stay organized, maintain consistency, and achieve their goals within a realistic timeframe. Whether someone is pursuing IT for career advancement, certification preparation, or personal development, a study plan provides direction and motivation to keep learning on track.

The first step in creating a study plan is defining clear and achievable goals. Learning IT is a continuous journey, and setting specific objectives helps learners measure progress and stay focused. Goals can be short-term, such as mastering the basics of a programming language or passing a certification exam, or long-term, like becoming a cybersecurity analyst or cloud engineer. Having a clear understanding of what needs to be accomplished allows individuals to break down complex topics into manageable learning milestones. Setting deadlines for each milestone also adds a sense of accountability and keeps motivation levels high.

Once goals are established, it is important to assess the current level of knowledge and identify skill gaps. IT learners come from different backgrounds, and understanding where they stand helps them determine which topics require more attention. Beginners who are new to IT may need to start with foundational concepts such as computer hardware, operating systems, and networking before diving into advanced subjects. Those with some experience may focus on specific skills like automation, cloud technologies, or security protocols. Conducting a self-assessment or taking an online quiz on IT fundamentals can help learners understand their strengths and weaknesses before structuring their study plan.

Selecting the right learning materials is a crucial aspect of an effective study plan. There are numerous free and paid resources available, including online courses, textbooks, video tutorials, interactive labs, and practice exams. Beginners should choose materials that align with their learning style, whether they prefer hands-on labs, reading textbooks, or watching instructional videos. Reliable platforms such as Coursera, Udemy, LinkedIn Learning, and Pluralsight offer structured courses on various IT topics. For hands-on experience, virtual labs, coding exercises, and cloud sandboxes provide practical exposure to real-world scenarios. Using a combination of resources enhances understanding and reinforces learning through multiple perspectives.

Time management plays a key role in IT learning, as consistent study habits lead to better retention and skill development. Creating a realistic study schedule based on available time and daily commitments ensures steady progress without burnout. Learners should allocate dedicated study hours each day or week, depending on their availability. It is more effective to study consistently for shorter periods than to cram information in a single session. For example, studying IT concepts for one or two hours daily is more productive than attempting to absorb large amounts of information in one sitting. Dividing study sessions into focused blocks with breaks in between helps maintain concentration and prevents mental fatigue.

A study plan should also include a balance between theory and practice. While understanding theoretical concepts is essential, hands-on practice is what solidifies knowledge in IT. Setting up a home lab, working on coding projects, or participating in cybersecurity challenges enhances technical skills and prepares learners for real-world tasks. Aspiring network administrators can use tools like Cisco Packet Tracer or GNS3 to simulate network configurations. Those learning programming can work on small coding projects, contribute to open-source repositories, or solve algorithm challenges. Cybersecurity enthusiasts can practice ethical hacking on platforms like TryHackMe or Hack The Box. Applying learned concepts in practical scenarios strengthens problem-solving skills and boosts confidence.

Tracking progress is another important component of an effective study plan. Keeping a journal, spreadsheet, or progress tracker helps learners stay motivated and evaluate their learning journey. Recording completed courses, achieved certifications, and hands-on projects provides a sense of accomplishment and highlights areas that need improvement. Reviewing progress regularly allows learners to adjust their study plan if necessary, ensuring that they stay on the right path. If certain topics are more challenging than expected, additional time can be allocated to reinforce those concepts before moving forward.

Joining IT communities and engaging with others in the field accelerates learning and provides valuable support. Online forums, social media groups, and local meetups offer opportunities to interact with experienced professionals and fellow learners. Platforms like Stack Overflow, Reddit's IT and cybersecurity communities, and LinkedIn groups allow individuals to ask questions, share knowledge, and learn from real-world experiences. Participating in discussions, attending webinars, and collaborating on projects create a dynamic learning environment that enhances understanding and provides networking opportunities. Being part of an IT community also helps learners stay updated with industry trends, new technologies, and best practices.

For those pursuing IT certifications, incorporating practice exams and review sessions into the study plan is essential. Certification exams often test not only theoretical knowledge but also practical problem-solving skills. Taking practice tests helps learners become familiar with exam formats, identify weak areas, and improve time management during exams. Official certification providers such as CompTIA, Cisco, AWS, and Microsoft offer practice exams that simulate real test conditions. Reviewing mistakes and revisiting difficult topics ensures thorough preparation before attempting the actual exam.

Staying motivated throughout the learning process is key to long-term success. IT learning can be challenging, especially when tackling complex topics such as networking protocols, cybersecurity threats, or software development frameworks. Setting small rewards for achieving milestones, celebrating progress, and reminding oneself of career aspirations can help maintain motivation. If frustration arises, taking short breaks, switching to different topics, or seeking guidance from experienced professionals can prevent discouragement. Viewing IT learning as a journey rather than a race encourages continuous improvement and adaptability to new challenges.

Adjusting the study plan as needed ensures that learning remains effective and relevant. Technology evolves rapidly, and IT professionals must adapt to changes by updating their skills and exploring emerging fields. Reviewing and modifying the study plan periodically allows learners to incorporate new topics, refine their focus, and align their learning path with industry demands. Flexibility in learning ensures that individuals remain competitive in the ever-changing IT landscape.

A well-structured study plan is essential for anyone looking to develop IT skills efficiently and achieve career goals. Defining clear objectives, selecting the right learning materials, managing time effectively, practicing hands-on skills, tracking progress, and engaging with the IT community all contribute to a successful learning journey. With dedication, consistency, and a strategic approach, individuals can build a strong foundation in IT and continuously advance their expertise in the field.

Hands-On Practice: Setting Up a Virtual Lab

One of the most effective ways to learn IT skills is through hands-on practice. Setting up a virtual lab provides a safe and controlled environment where individuals can experiment with operating systems, networking configurations, security tools, and programming without the risk of damaging real systems. A virtual lab is particularly beneficial for those who want to gain practical experience in system administration, cybersecurity, ethical hacking, cloud computing, and software development. By creating a virtual environment, learners can test different scenarios, troubleshoot issues, and develop problem-solving skills that are essential for IT professionals.

A virtual lab is typically created using virtualization software that allows multiple operating systems to run on a single physical machine. Virtualization technology enables users to install and operate different operating systems in isolated environments without affecting their main system. Some of the most popular virtualization tools include VirtualBox, VMware Workstation, and Hyper-V. These tools provide the flexibility to create, modify, and delete virtual machines (VMs) as needed. VirtualBox is a free, open-source option that is widely used by beginners, while VMware Workstation offers advanced features for professional environments. Hyper-V, which is built into Windows, is a powerful tool for users who want to work with virtual machines without installing third-party software.

Once a virtualization platform is selected, the next step is to install and configure virtual machines. The most commonly used operating systems in virtual labs are Windows, Linux, and specialized cybersecurity distributions such as Kali Linux. Installing different operating systems allows learners to familiarize themselves with their interfaces, command-line utilities, and administrative tools. Many Linux distributions, including Ubuntu, Debian, and CentOS, are free to download and widely used in enterprise environments. Windows Server editions are also valuable for learning system administration, domain management, and Active Directory configuration. By setting up multiple virtual machines, users can simulate networked environments and practice configuring connections between systems.

Networking is an essential component of IT, and a virtual lab provides the perfect opportunity to practice configuring and troubleshooting network settings. Virtual machines can be connected through internal networks, allowing learners to set up local area networks (LANs) and experiment with IP addressing, subnetting, and routing. Using tools such as Cisco Packet Tracer and GNS3, individuals can design and simulate complex network topologies that include routers, switches, and firewalls. These networking simulations help learners understand how data flows between devices, how network security measures are implemented, and how to diagnose connectivity issues. Setting up a virtual lab for networking practice is an excellent way to prepare for certifications such as Cisco's CCNA or CompTIA Network+.

For cybersecurity enthusiasts, a virtual lab is an essential tool for practicing ethical hacking, penetration testing, and digital forensics. Kali Linux, a popular cybersecurity distribution, comes preloaded with penetration testing tools such as Metasploit, Nmap, Wireshark, and Burp Suite. By setting up a target machine, such as Metasploitable or DVWA (Damn Vulnerable Web Application), learners can practice vulnerability assessments and exploit simulations in a controlled environment. Practicing cybersecurity techniques in a virtual lab ensures that skills are developed ethically and legally, without violating security policies or laws. Many cybersecurity professionals use virtual labs to test new tools, analyze malware behavior, and improve their incident response skills.

For those interested in cloud computing, a virtual lab can be extended to include cloud services from platforms such as Amazon Web Services (AWS), Microsoft Azure, and Google Cloud. Many cloud providers offer free-tier accounts that allow users to set up virtual machines, deploy applications, and configure cloud networking. Learning how to manage virtual environments in the cloud provides valuable experience for IT professionals looking to work in DevOps, cloud administration, and cloud security. Connecting local virtual machines with cloud-based services enhances the learning experience and provides a real-world understanding of hybrid cloud architectures.

Programming and automation can also be practiced within a virtual lab. Setting up a virtual environment for coding allows developers to experiment with different programming languages, frameworks, and automation scripts without affecting their main operating system. Python, Bash scripting, and PowerShell are commonly used for automating administrative tasks, managing system configurations, and performing security operations. Developers can install Integrated Development Environments (IDEs) such as VS Code, PyCharm, or Eclipse on their virtual machines to build and test software applications. Automating repetitive tasks in a virtual lab provides a deeper understanding of scripting and its role in IT operations.

Maintaining a virtual lab requires managing system resources efficiently. Running multiple virtual machines simultaneously can consume a significant amount of CPU, RAM, and disk space. Allocating sufficient resources to each virtual machine ensures smooth performance and prevents system crashes. Users can optimize performance by adjusting VM settings, using snapshots to save system states, and deleting unused virtual machines when they are no longer needed. Regular updates to the operating systems and installed software help keep the virtual lab secure and functional. Learning how to troubleshoot common virtualization issues, such as network conflicts or disk space limitations, enhances technical problem-solving skills.

Documenting experiments and configurations in a virtual lab is a good practice that helps learners track their progress and retain knowledge. Keeping a log of system settings, commands used, and issues encountered can serve as a valuable reference for future troubleshooting and learning. Writing down step-by-step procedures for tasks such as setting up a firewall, configuring a web server, or deploying a database can reinforce understanding and make it easier to replicate processes in real-world scenarios. Creating documentation also prepares learners for IT roles that require technical writing and reporting skills.

Virtual labs are widely used by IT professionals, students, and researchers because they provide a risk-free environment for testing new technologies and developing expertise. Many certification training programs and IT courses encourage learners to build virtual labs to complement theoretical learning with practical application. Employers value hands-on experience, and having a well-structured virtual lab demonstrates initiative and technical proficiency. Including virtual lab projects in a portfolio can help job seekers showcase their practical skills and problem-solving abilities to potential employers.

Setting up a virtual lab is one of the best ways to gain real-world IT experience without expensive hardware or the risk of misconfiguring production systems. Whether learning networking, cybersecurity, cloud computing, or programming, a virtual lab provides a flexible and scalable environment for experimentation and skill development. By continuously using and refining the lab setup, IT learners can improve their technical abilities, gain confidence, and prepare for professional certifications and job roles in the IT industry.

Understanding Cloud Computing Basics

Cloud computing has revolutionized the way businesses and individuals store, process, and manage data. It provides a scalable, on-demand computing environment that eliminates the need for traditional on-premises infrastructure. By leveraging cloud services, organizations can reduce costs, increase efficiency, and access computing power without having to invest in expensive hardware. Understanding the basics of cloud computing is essential for anyone looking to work in IT, as more companies are adopting cloud technologies for hosting applications, managing databases, and improving collaboration.

At its core, cloud computing refers to the delivery of computing services over the internet. These services include servers, storage, databases, networking, software, and analytics, all hosted on remote data centers managed by cloud providers. Instead of maintaining physical infrastructure, users can access and use these resources on a pay-as-you-go basis. This model allows businesses to scale their operations quickly, reducing the need for upfront capital expenditures. Cloud computing is widely used in various industries, from healthcare and finance to entertainment and e-commerce.

Cloud computing is categorized into three main service models: Infrastructure as a Service (IaaS), Platform as a Service (PaaS), and Software as a Service (SaaS). Each model serves a different purpose and provides varying levels of control over computing resources.

Infrastructure as a Service (IaaS) is the most flexible cloud computing model, providing virtualized computing resources such as virtual machines, storage, and networking. With IaaS, users can deploy and manage their own operating systems, applications, and databases on cloud-based servers. This model is ideal for businesses that require complete control over their IT infrastructure without the burden of maintaining physical hardware. Popular IaaS providers include

Amazon Web Services (AWS), Microsoft Azure, and Google Cloud Platform (GCP). Organizations use IaaS to host websites, run enterprise applications, and manage big data workloads.

Platform as a Service (PaaS) offers a cloud-based environment for developers to build, test, and deploy applications without worrying about managing the underlying infrastructure. PaaS solutions provide pre-configured platforms that include operating systems, development tools, and database management systems. This model simplifies software development by allowing developers to focus on writing code rather than dealing with server maintenance and configurations. Examples of PaaS offerings include Google App Engine, Microsoft Azure App Services, and AWS Elastic Beanstalk. PaaS is widely used for web and mobile application development, enabling faster deployment and continuous integration of software updates.

Software as a Service (SaaS) is the most user-friendly cloud computing model, delivering fully functional applications over the internet. Instead of installing software on local computers, users access SaaS applications through web browsers. SaaS eliminates the need for software maintenance, updates, and security patches, as the cloud provider handles these tasks. Common examples of SaaS applications include Google Workspace (formerly G Suite), Microsoft 365, Dropbox, and Salesforce. SaaS is widely used for email services, collaboration tools, customer relationship management (CRM), and enterprise resource planning (ERP). Businesses and individuals rely on SaaS applications for productivity, communication, and data management.

Cloud computing also offers different deployment models to meet the needs of various organizations. These models include public cloud, private cloud, hybrid cloud, and multi-cloud environments.

The public cloud is the most common deployment model, where computing resources are shared among multiple users and managed by a third-party provider. Public cloud services are cost-effective and highly scalable, making them suitable for startups, small businesses, and organizations with fluctuating workloads. Companies such as Amazon, Microsoft, and Google operate massive public cloud infrastructures that provide services to businesses and individuals worldwide. Public cloud users benefit from the provider's expertise in security, reliability, and performance optimization.

The private cloud is a dedicated cloud environment used exclusively by a single organization. Unlike the public cloud, a private cloud is not shared with other users, providing greater control, security, and compliance. Organizations that handle sensitive data, such as financial institutions and government agencies, often choose private cloud solutions to meet regulatory requirements. A private cloud can be hosted on-premises within a company's data center or managed by a third-party provider. While private clouds offer enhanced security and customization, they require higher investments in infrastructure and maintenance.

A hybrid cloud combines elements of both public and private clouds, allowing organizations to distribute workloads across different environments. This model provides greater flexibility by enabling businesses to use the public cloud for less sensitive operations while keeping critical data and applications in a private cloud. Hybrid cloud strategies are popular among enterprises that need to balance scalability with security and compliance. Cloud providers such as AWS, Azure, and Google Cloud offer hybrid cloud solutions that integrate on-premises infrastructure with cloud-based services.

A multi-cloud approach involves using multiple cloud providers to meet specific business needs. Companies adopt multi-cloud strategies to avoid vendor lock-in, improve redundancy, and take advantage of specialized services from different providers. For example, an organization might use AWS for storage, Azure for artificial intelligence capabilities, and Google Cloud for big data analytics. Managing a multi-cloud environment requires careful planning to ensure seamless integration and cost optimization.

Cloud security is a critical aspect of cloud computing, as organizations must protect their data and applications from cyber threats. Cloud providers implement robust security measures, including encryption, identity and access management (IAM), and compliance certifications. However, users also have a responsibility to secure their cloud environments by configuring access controls, monitoring network traffic, and implementing best practices for data protection. Cloud security frameworks such as the Shared Responsibility Model outline the security obligations of both the provider and the user. Understanding cloud security principles is essential for IT professionals working in cloud administration and cybersecurity roles.

One of the biggest advantages of cloud computing is its scalability. Organizations can quickly adjust their computing resources based on demand, ensuring cost efficiency and optimal performance. Autoscaling features allow cloud applications to handle increased workloads automatically, preventing service disruptions during peak usage periods. This scalability makes cloud computing ideal for businesses that experience seasonal traffic spikes, such as e-commerce platforms and streaming services.

Cloud computing also enhances collaboration by enabling remote access to applications and data from anywhere with an internet connection. Cloud-based storage solutions such as Google Drive, OneDrive, and Dropbox allow teams to share files and work on documents in real time. Cloud collaboration tools like Slack, Microsoft Teams, and Zoom have become essential for remote work, allowing employees to communicate and coordinate projects seamlessly. The ability to access cloud resources from any location has transformed the way businesses operate, making IT infrastructure more flexible and accessible.

Understanding cloud computing basics is essential for IT professionals looking to work in cloud administration, cybersecurity, or software development. As more organizations migrate to the cloud, the demand for cloud computing expertise continues to grow. Gaining hands-on experience with cloud platforms through free-tier accounts, certifications, and virtual labs provides valuable skills that are highly sought after in the IT job market. By learning how cloud computing works, individuals can leverage its benefits to optimize business operations, improve security, and enhance their career opportunities in the technology industry.

Learning the Fundamentals of IT Support

IT support is one of the most critical areas in information technology, as it ensures that computer systems, networks, and software function smoothly for businesses and individuals. IT support professionals are responsible for troubleshooting technical issues, assisting users, maintaining hardware and software, and ensuring overall system efficiency. For many aspiring IT professionals, starting a career in IT support is an excellent entry point into the industry, providing hands-on experience with technology and the opportunity to develop problem-solving skills. Understanding the fundamentals of IT support is essential for those looking to enter this field, as it requires technical knowledge, communication skills, and the ability to diagnose and resolve a wide range of computer-related problems.

IT support is often categorized into different levels based on complexity and specialization. Tier 1 support, also known as help desk support, is the first point of contact for users experiencing technical issues. Tier 1 professionals handle common problems such as password resets, software installations, and basic troubleshooting. If the issue cannot be resolved at this level, it is escalated to Tier 2 support, where more experienced technicians analyze and fix more complex hardware or software issues. Tier 3 support consists of specialized IT experts who deal with advanced system failures, software bugs, and network infrastructure problems. Understanding these levels helps IT professionals determine which skills they need to develop as they progress in their careers.

A strong foundation in computer hardware is essential for IT support professionals, as many technical issues involve diagnosing and repairing physical components. Understanding how central processing units (CPUs), memory (RAM), hard drives, motherboards, and power supplies function allows technicians to identify hardware failures and recommend appropriate solutions. Many IT support roles involve assembling and disassembling computers, replacing faulty components, and upgrading systems to improve performance. Familiarity with different types of storage devices, such as solid-state drives (SSDs) and hard disk drives (HDDs), is also important for resolving storage-related issues.

Operating system knowledge is another fundamental aspect of IT support. Most organizations use a combination of Windows, macOS, and Linux, and support technicians must be comfortable troubleshooting all three operating systems. Common tasks include configuring system settings, installing updates, managing drivers, and addressing performance issues. Windows is the most widely used operating system in business environments, making it crucial for IT support professionals to understand its features, including Active Directory, group policies, and user account management. Linux is widely used in servers and development environments, requiring familiarity with the command line, file permissions, and basic shell scripting. macOS is prevalent in creative industries and education, requiring IT support technicians to understand Apple's system architecture, troubleshooting tools, and integration with other Apple devices.

Networking knowledge is also vital for IT support professionals, as connectivity issues are one of the most common problems users face. Understanding the basics of TCP/IP, DNS, DHCP, and subnetting helps technicians diagnose network problems and restore connectivity. IT support professionals should know how to configure routers, troubleshoot wireless connections, and set up virtual private networks (VPNs) for remote users. Familiarity with network diagnostic tools such as ping, traceroute, and netstat allows technicians to identify connection issues and resolve them efficiently. Many businesses use enterprise networking equipment from vendors such as Cisco and Juniper, making certifications such as CompTIA Network+ or Cisco's CCNA valuable for IT support professionals looking to advance in networking roles.

Customer service and communication skills are just as important as technical expertise in IT support. Support technicians must be able to explain technical concepts to non-technical users, ensuring they understand the problem and its resolution. Patience and professionalism are essential when dealing with frustrated users who may not have a strong technical background. Effective communication involves active listening, asking the right questions to diagnose issues, and providing clear instructions for troubleshooting steps. IT support professionals must also document their work, keeping records of support tickets, solutions, and system changes for future reference.

Security awareness is another crucial component of IT support. Technicians often handle sensitive data and must ensure that security best practices are followed. IT support professionals play a role in enforcing password policies, managing user access, and identifying potential security threats. Common security practices include setting up multi-factor authentication (MFA), implementing encryption, and educating users about phishing attacks. Many IT support teams work closely with cybersecurity specialists to prevent data breaches and maintain system integrity. Understanding basic security concepts helps IT support technicians contribute to an organization's overall cybersecurity strategy.

Troubleshooting methodology is an essential skill for IT support professionals, as diagnosing technical issues requires a logical and systematic approach. The first step in troubleshooting is gathering information about the problem by asking the user detailed questions and replicating the issue when possible. Next, technicians analyze potential causes, test solutions, and document their findings. If the problem cannot be resolved at the initial level, it is escalated to a higher-tier technician with more specialized knowledge. Developing a structured approach to problem-solving ensures that issues are resolved efficiently and reduces downtime for users and businesses.

IT support professionals also work with various software applications, including productivity tools, enterprise applications, and remote support software. Familiarity with Microsoft Office, Google Workspace, and enterprise resource planning (ERP) systems helps technicians assist users with common software-related issues. Remote desktop applications such as TeamViewer, AnyDesk, and Windows Remote Desktop Protocol (RDP) allow support technicians to troubleshoot problems without being physically present. Ticketing systems such as ServiceNow, Zendesk, and Freshdesk are used to manage support requests, track issue resolution times, and prioritize tasks. Learning how to use these tools efficiently improves productivity and enhances the support experience for users.

Many IT support roles require certifications that validate technical skills and knowledge. The CompTIA A+ certification is one of the most widely recognized credentials for entry-level IT support professionals. It covers hardware, operating systems, troubleshooting, networking, and security fundamentals. Other valuable certifications include ITIL Foundation for IT service management, CompTIA Network+ for networking fundamentals, and Microsoft's certifications for Windows administration. Earning certifications demonstrates competence and commitment to professional development, making job candidates more competitive in the IT job market.

Career growth in IT support is possible through continuous learning and gaining hands-on experience. Many professionals start in entry-level help desk positions and advance to specialized roles in system administration, networking, or cybersecurity. Developing additional skills in scripting, automation, and cloud computing can open doors to higher-paying positions and greater responsibilities. IT support provides a strong foundation for understanding how IT systems work, making it an ideal starting point for a long-term career in technology. By gaining experience, earning certifications, and refining both technical and customer service skills, IT support professionals can progress into more advanced IT roles and contribute to the success of their organizations.

Getting Started with Networking and TCP/IP

Networking is the foundation of modern communication, enabling devices, applications, and users to share information efficiently. Every aspect of the internet, from browsing websites to sending emails and streaming videos, depends on networking technologies. Understanding how networks function is crucial for anyone entering the IT field, as networking plays a vital role in system administration, cybersecurity, cloud computing, and software development. One of the most fundamental concepts in networking is the TCP/IP protocol suite, which defines how data is transmitted across networks and ensures reliable communication between devices.

A computer network is a collection of interconnected devices that exchange data using established rules, known as protocols. These devices include computers, servers, routers, switches, and other networking hardware. Networks can be categorized based on their size and purpose, such as local area networks (LANs), wide area networks (WANs), and wireless networks. A LAN connects devices within a limited area, such as an office, home, or campus, using wired or wireless connections. A WAN, on the other hand, spans a larger geographical area and connects multiple LANs together, often using telecommunications infrastructure. The internet is the largest example of a WAN, linking millions of networks worldwide.

The TCP/IP model, which stands for Transmission Control Protocol/Internet Protocol, is the backbone of modern networking. It is a set of rules that dictate how data is sent, received, and processed across the internet and local networks. The TCP/IP model is structured into four layers, each responsible for different aspects of communication. The application layer handles high-level services such as web browsing, email, and file transfers. The transport layer ensures reliable data transmission through protocols like TCP and UDP. The internet layer is responsible for routing data packets across networks using IP addressing. The network access layer deals with the physical transmission of data over cables, Wi-Fi, and other networking mediums.

IP addressing is a fundamental concept in networking, as it allows devices to be uniquely identified on a network. Every device connected to a network has an IP address, which serves as its digital identifier. There are two versions of IP addresses: IPv4 and IPv6. IPv4 addresses consist of four sets of numbers separated by dots, such as 192.168.1.1. Due to the growing number of internet-connected devices, IPv6 was introduced to provide a larger address space, using a hexadecimal format such as 2001:0db8:85a3::8a2e:0370:7334. Understanding how IP addressing works, along with subnetting, enables network administrators to efficiently manage and allocate IP addresses within an organization.

Subnetting is the process of dividing a network into smaller segments, or subnets, to improve efficiency and security. Subnet masks determine which portion of an IP address belongs to the network and which part identifies individual devices. For example, the subnet mask 255.255.255.0 indicates that the first three octets of an IPv4 address represent the network, while the last octet is assigned to individual devices. Subnetting reduces network congestion, optimizes bandwidth usage, and enhances security by isolating different departments or user groups within an organization. Network professionals use subnetting to design scalable and organized network architectures.

Routing is another essential networking concept that ensures data packets travel efficiently from one device to another. Routers play a key role in directing traffic between networks, determining the best path for data transmission. When a user visits a website, the request travels through multiple routers before reaching the destination server. Routing protocols, such as RIP, OSPF, and BGP, help routers make intelligent decisions about forwarding data. OSPF (Open Shortest Path First) is commonly used in enterprise networks to find the shortest route between devices, while BGP (Border Gateway Protocol) manages internet-wide routing between different service providers.

The Domain Name System (DNS) is a crucial component of networking, translating human-readable domain names into IP addresses. When a user types a website address like www.example.com into a browser, DNS servers convert it into the corresponding IP address so that the request can be directed to the correct server. Without DNS, users would have to remember complex numerical IP addresses instead of simple domain names. DNS servers operate in a hierarchical structure, with root servers at the top, followed by top-level domain (TLD) servers, and authoritative name servers that store domain-specific records. Understanding how DNS works is essential for network administrators, as incorrect configurations can lead to website downtime and connectivity issues.

Network security is a critical aspect of networking, ensuring that data is protected from unauthorized access, attacks, and breaches. Firewalls are one of the primary security measures used to filter incoming and outgoing traffic based on predefined rules. They can be hardware-based or software-based and help block malicious activity, unauthorized access attempts, and harmful network traffic. Intrusion detection systems (IDS) and intrusion prevention systems (IPS) provide additional layers of security by monitoring network activity for signs of suspicious behavior and taking action to prevent potential threats. Implementing strong security measures, such as encryption, secure authentication, and access controls, helps protect networks from cyber threats.

Network troubleshooting is a valuable skill for IT professionals, as connectivity issues are common in any organization. Basic troubleshooting involves checking physical connections, verifying IP configurations, and using diagnostic tools to identify problems. Commands such as ping, tracert, and netstat help network administrators diagnose connectivity issues and latency problems. Ping tests whether a device is reachable on the network, while tracert maps the route taken by data packets to reach a destination. Understanding these tools and techniques allows IT professionals to quickly resolve network problems and maintain system reliability.

Wireless networking has become increasingly important, as Wi-Fi enables seamless connectivity for mobile devices, laptops, and smart appliances. Wireless networks use radio waves to transmit data, with standards such as IEEE 802.11 defining Wi-Fi protocols. Encryption methods like WPA2 and WPA3 ensure that wireless communications remain secure and protected from eavesdropping. Setting up and maintaining a secure wireless network requires configuring access points, managing bandwidth allocation, and preventing unauthorized connections. IT professionals responsible for networking must understand how to optimize wireless performance, troubleshoot signal interference, and enforce security policies to protect sensitive data.

Learning the fundamentals of networking and TCP/IP is essential for anyone entering the IT field. Networks power the digital world, enabling communication, business operations, and technological advancements. Gaining practical experience by setting up home labs, configuring routers and switches, and experimenting with different networking tools helps reinforce theoretical knowledge. As technology continues to evolve, networking professionals must stay updated with new protocols, security best practices, and cloud-based networking solutions. A strong foundation in networking principles opens up opportunities in various IT careers, including network administration, cybersecurity, and cloud computing.

Basics of Databases and SQL

Databases are an essential component of modern technology, enabling the storage, retrieval, and management of vast amounts of structured information. Nearly every application, from websites and mobile apps to enterprise software and cloud services, relies on databases to store user data, transaction records, and business information. Understanding how databases work and how to interact with them using SQL (Structured Query Language) is a fundamental skill for IT professionals, developers, and data analysts. Whether managing a small database for a personal project or working with complex enterprise systems, knowledge of databases and SQL is invaluable in handling data efficiently.

A database is a structured collection of data organized in a way that allows efficient storage, retrieval, and modification. Traditional databases are relational, meaning that data is stored in tables with predefined relationships between them. Each table consists of rows, known as records, and columns, known as fields, where each field represents a specific attribute of the data. For example, a customer database might contain a table with columns for customer ID, name, email, and phone number, while each row stores details for an individual customer. Relational databases follow a strict schema, ensuring that data is consistent and well-structured.

SQL, or Structured Query Language, is the standard language used to interact with relational databases. It allows users to perform a wide range of operations, including retrieving data, inserting new records, updating existing information, and deleting unwanted data. SQL follows a declarative syntax, meaning that users specify what they want to accomplish rather than how the database should execute the operation. SQL statements are executed by database management systems (DBMS) such as MySQL, PostgreSQL, Microsoft SQL Server, and Oracle Database. Each of these systems provides tools for managing databases, optimizing performance, and ensuring data security.

One of the most fundamental SQL commands is the SELECT statement, which is used to retrieve data from a database. A basic SELECT query retrieves all records from a table, displaying the information stored within it. For example, the command SELECT * FROM customers; retrieves all columns and rows from the "customers" table. To narrow down the results, the WHERE clause can be used to filter data based on specific conditions. If a user wants to find all customers from a specific city, they can use SELECT * FROM customers WHERE city = 'New York';. This query returns only the records where the city field matches "New York."

In addition to retrieving data, SQL allows users to modify records using the INSERT, UPDATE, and DELETE statements. The INSERT statement adds new records to a table. For example, INSERT INTO customers (name, email, city) VALUES ('John Doe', 'john@example.com', 'Los Angeles'); inserts a new customer into the database. The UPDATE statement modifies existing records, allowing users to change values based on conditions. To update a customer's email address, the query UPDATE customers SET email = 'newemail@example.com' WHERE name = 'John Doe'; modifies the relevant record. If data needs to be removed, the DELETE statement is used. The command DELETE FROM customers WHERE name = 'John Doe'; removes the specified record from the table.

Databases often contain multiple related tables, and SQL provides powerful tools for joining data from different sources. The JOIN operation allows users to retrieve data from multiple tables based on a common field. For example, if a business has a "customers" table and an "orders" table, they can use an INNER JOIN to retrieve all orders placed by a specific customer. The query SELECT customers.name, orders.order_id FROM customers INNER JOIN orders ON customers.customer_id = orders.customer_id; combines information from both tables, ensuring that only matching records are displayed. Other types of joins, such as LEFT JOIN and RIGHT JOIN, allow users to retrieve data even if one of the tables does not have a matching record.

Data integrity is a crucial aspect of database management, ensuring that stored information remains accurate and consistent. Primary keys and foreign keys are used to maintain relationships between tables. A primary key is a unique identifier for each record in a table, ensuring that no duplicate entries exist. For example, the "customers" table may use "customer_id" as its primary key. A foreign key is a reference to a primary key in another table, establishing relationships between records. In an "orders" table, "customer_id" might be a foreign key linking each order to a specific customer. Enforcing these relationships prevents data inconsistencies and improves database reliability.

Indexing is another important database concept that improves query performance. An index is a data structure that speeds up searches by allowing the database to locate records more efficiently. Without indexes, the database must scan every row in a table to find matching results, which can be slow for large datasets. Creating an index on frequently searched columns, such as CREATE INDEX idx_customer_email ON customers(email);, improves query speed and enhances overall performance. However, excessive indexing can slow down data insertion and updates, so database administrators must carefully balance performance optimizations.

Transactions play a vital role in database operations, ensuring that data modifications are completed safely and reliably. A transaction is a sequence of operations that must be executed as a single unit, following the ACID properties: Atomicity, Consistency, Isolation, and Durability. Atomicity ensures that either all operations within a transaction are completed successfully or none are applied. Consistency maintains database integrity before and after a transaction. Isolation prevents concurrent transactions from interfering with each other. Durability ensures that once a transaction is committed, it remains stored even in the event of a system failure. Database management systems provide transaction controls such as BEGIN, COMMIT, and ROLLBACK to manage data consistency.

Security is a fundamental concern in database management, as unauthorized access to sensitive data can lead to serious consequences. SQL provides mechanisms for user authentication and access control. Database administrators can create user accounts and assign permissions to restrict actions based on roles. For example, a database user may have read-only access to customer records but not be allowed to modify or delete them. The command GRANT SELECT ON customers TO user_readonly; grants read-only access to a specific user. Encryption techniques, firewalls, and backup strategies further enhance database security, protecting against data breaches and system failures.

Understanding databases and SQL is a valuable skill for IT professionals, as businesses rely on data-driven decision-making and efficient information management. Mastering SQL allows individuals to retrieve, manipulate, and analyze data effectively, supporting software development, business intelligence, and system administration. Practical experience with SQL queries, database design, and optimization techniques helps professionals build robust and scalable data solutions. As technology continues to evolve, knowledge of databases remains essential for working with applications, cloud computing, and data science, making it one of the most important areas of expertise in the IT industry.

Understanding Cybersecurity Fundamentals

Cybersecurity is one of the most critical areas in IT, as it focuses on protecting systems, networks, and data from cyber threats. As organizations and individuals rely more on digital technologies, the risk of cyberattacks has increased, making cybersecurity an essential field for IT professionals. Understanding the fundamentals of cybersecurity is necessary for anyone looking to work in IT, as security principles apply to every aspect of technology, from software development and network administration to cloud computing and data management. Without proper security measures, businesses and individuals are vulnerable to data breaches, identity theft, and system compromises that can result in significant financial and reputational damage.

Cybersecurity is based on three core principles known as the CIA triad: Confidentiality, Integrity, and Availability. Confidentiality ensures that data is accessible only to authorized individuals and is protected from unauthorized access. Integrity guarantees that data remains accurate and unaltered, preventing unauthorized modifications. Availability ensures that systems and data remain accessible to authorized users when needed, preventing disruptions caused by cyberattacks or system failures. These three principles form the foundation of cybersecurity strategies and guide the implementation of security measures across different IT environments.

One of the most common cybersecurity threats is malware, which refers to malicious software designed to harm or exploit computer systems. Malware comes in many forms, including viruses, worms, trojans, ransomware, and spyware. Viruses attach themselves to legitimate programs and spread when executed, while worms replicate independently and spread across networks. Trojans disguise themselves as harmless applications but perform malicious actions in the background. Ransomware encrypts files and demands payment from victims in exchange for decryption keys. Spyware secretly collects information about users and their activities. To protect against malware, organizations and individuals use antivirus software, firewalls, and endpoint protection solutions to detect and remove threats before they cause damage.

Phishing is another major cybersecurity threat that targets individuals through deceptive emails, messages, or websites. Attackers impersonate legitimate entities to trick victims into providing sensitive information such as passwords, credit card details, or personal identification numbers. Phishing attacks often use social engineering techniques to create a sense of urgency, making users more likely to fall for the scam. Common phishing tactics include fraudulent emails pretending to be from banks, online retailers, or government agencies. To defend against phishing, individuals should verify the authenticity of messages, avoid clicking on suspicious links, and enable multi-factor authentication (MFA) to add an extra layer of security.

Network security is a crucial aspect of cybersecurity, as many cyberattacks target network vulnerabilities to gain unauthorized access. Firewalls are one of the primary defenses used to filter incoming and outgoing traffic, blocking malicious activity while allowing legitimate communication. Intrusion Detection Systems (IDS) and Intrusion Prevention Systems (IPS) monitor network activity for signs of suspicious behavior and take action to prevent potential threats. Secure network configurations, such as encrypting data transmissions using protocols like SSL/TLS and implementing Virtual Private

Networks (VPNs), help protect sensitive information from interception by attackers. IT professionals working in network administration must ensure that security policies are enforced to prevent unauthorized access and data breaches.

User authentication and access control are fundamental security measures that protect systems and data from unauthorized users. Authentication verifies the identity of users before granting access, typically using passwords, biometrics, smart cards, or authentication tokens. Multi-factor authentication (MFA) enhances security by requiring users to provide multiple forms of verification, such as a password and a temporary code sent to a mobile device. Access control mechanisms determine what actions users are allowed to perform based on their roles and privileges. The principle of least privilege (PoLP) states that users should have only the minimum level of access necessary to perform their tasks, reducing the risk of unauthorized activities or accidental data exposure.

Encryption is a vital cybersecurity technique that protects data by converting it into an unreadable format that can only be decrypted with the correct key. Encryption is used to secure communications, protect sensitive information stored on devices, and ensure the integrity of transmitted data. Common encryption methods include symmetric encryption, where the same key is used for encryption and decryption, and asymmetric encryption, which uses a pair of public and private keys. Secure communication protocols such as HTTPS, SSH, and TLS rely on encryption to prevent data interception and unauthorized access. Businesses and organizations use encryption to safeguard customer data, financial transactions, and confidential documents from cybercriminals.

Cybersecurity also involves securing operating systems and applications from vulnerabilities that attackers can exploit. Software developers and IT administrators regularly release patches and updates to fix security flaws and improve system defenses. Failing to install updates can leave systems exposed to known vulnerabilities that cybercriminals can use to gain access. Patch management is an essential practice that ensures all software and hardware components are up to date with the latest security fixes. Organizations often implement automated patch management systems to reduce the risk of security gaps caused by outdated software.

Social engineering is a tactic used by attackers to manipulate individuals into revealing confidential information or performing actions that compromise security. Unlike technical cyberattacks, social engineering exploits human psychology to gain unauthorized access to systems or data. Common social engineering attacks include pretexting, where attackers create a fake scenario to deceive victims, and baiting, where malicious USB drives or downloads are used to trick users into installing malware. IT professionals and employees must be trained to recognize social engineering tactics and verify requests for sensitive information before responding. Security awareness training is essential in preventing human error, which remains one of the weakest links in cybersecurity.

Incident response is a key component of cybersecurity that involves detecting, investigating, and mitigating security incidents. Organizations develop incident response plans to outline the steps to take when a security breach occurs. The response process typically includes identifying the threat, containing the damage, eradicating the attacker's presence, recovering affected systems, and analyzing the incident to prevent future attacks. Cybersecurity professionals use forensic analysis tools to investigate security breaches and determine how attackers gained access. Regular security audits and penetration testing help identify vulnerabilities before they can be exploited by real attackers.

Cybersecurity is a constantly evolving field, as cyber threats continue to grow in sophistication. IT professionals must stay updated with the latest security trends, threat intelligence, and best practices to protect organizations from cyber risks. Certifications such as CompTIA Security+, Certified Ethical Hacker (CEH), and Certified Information Systems Security Professional (CISSP) provide valuable knowledge and credentials for individuals pursuing a career in cybersecurity. Gaining hands-on experience with security tools, participating in ethical hacking challenges, and practicing defensive strategies in virtual labs help develop practical skills that are essential for securing digital environments.

Understanding cybersecurity fundamentals is critical for anyone working in IT, as security affects every aspect of technology. Implementing security best practices, staying vigilant against threats, and continuously improving security skills help protect systems, data, and users from cyberattacks. Cybersecurity is a shared responsibility, requiring collaboration between IT professionals, businesses, and individuals to create a safer digital world.

Introduction to Web Development

Web development is the process of creating websites and web applications that users can access through a web browser. It is one of the most in-demand skills in the IT industry, as businesses, organizations, and individuals increasingly rely on the internet to communicate, provide services, and sell products. Web development combines creativity, problem-solving, and technical expertise to build functional and visually appealing websites. Whether a developer is working on a simple blog, an e-commerce platform, or a complex web application, understanding the fundamentals of web development is essential for creating interactive and dynamic online experiences.

Web development consists of two main areas: front-end development and back-end development. Front-end development focuses on the visual and interactive aspects of a website, while back-end development handles the server-side logic, databases, and application functionality. Full-stack development refers to the ability to work on both the front-end and back-end, making a developer proficient in all aspects of web development. Understanding the relationship between the front-end and back-end helps developers build efficient, responsive, and scalable web applications.

Front-end development involves creating the layout, design, and interactive features of a website. It primarily relies on three core technologies: HTML, CSS, and JavaScript. HTML, or HyperText Markup Language, provides the structure of a web page by defining elements such as headings, paragraphs, images, and links. CSS, or Cascading Style Sheets, controls the appearance of web pages, including colors, fonts, layouts, and animations. JavaScript is a programming language that adds interactivity to web pages, enabling features such as form validation, dynamic content updates, and animations. Modern front-end development also includes frameworks and libraries such as React, Angular, and Vue.js, which simplify the process of building complex user interfaces.

Responsive web design is an important aspect of front-end development, ensuring that websites look and function properly on different devices and screen sizes. With the growing use of mobile devices, developers must create web pages that adapt to various screen resolutions and orientations. Techniques such as flexible grid layouts, media queries, and scalable images help make websites responsive. Frameworks like Bootstrap provide pre-designed components and responsive grid systems that speed up development while maintaining a consistent design across devices. By mastering responsive design principles, developers can ensure that users have a seamless browsing experience, whether on a desktop, tablet, or smartphone.

Back-end development focuses on the server-side logic that powers web applications. It involves handling user requests, processing data, and managing databases. Back-end developers use programming languages such as Python, PHP, Java, Ruby, and JavaScript (Node.js) to create the logic that connects the front-end with the database and other services. A back-end application typically consists of a web server, an application layer, and a database. The web server processes requests from the user's browser and sends responses, while the application layer executes business logic, such as user authentication and data processing.

Databases play a crucial role in web development by storing and retrieving data used by web applications. There are two main types of databases: relational and non-relational. Relational databases, such as MySQL, PostgreSQL, and Microsoft SQL Server, store data in tables with structured relationships between them. Non-relational databases, such as MongoDB and Firebase, use flexible document-based storage, making them ideal for applications with dynamic and unstructured data. Back-end developers use SQL (Structured Query Language) to interact with relational databases, while NoSQL databases rely on different querying methods. Efficient database management ensures that web applications can store, retrieve, and manipulate data effectively.

APIs, or Application Programming Interfaces, are essential in web development, allowing different systems and services to communicate with each other. Developers use APIs to connect web applications to external services such as payment gateways, social media platforms, and cloud storage providers. REST (Representational State Transfer) and GraphQL are common API architectures used to structure and manage data exchange between front-end and back-end components. REST APIs use HTTP methods such as GET, POST, PUT, and DELETE to perform actions on data, while GraphQL provides a more flexible way to request specific data. APIs enable web applications to integrate with third-party services and enhance their functionality.

Web security is an important consideration in web development, as websites and web applications are frequent targets for cyberattacks. Developers must implement security measures to protect user data, prevent unauthorized access, and mitigate common threats. Secure authentication methods, such as hashing passwords and using multi-factor authentication, help protect user accounts. Encryption techniques, such as SSL/TLS certificates, ensure secure data transmission between the user's browser and the web server. Common security vulnerabilities, such as SQL injection, cross-site scripting (XSS), and cross-site request forgery (CSRF), must be addressed through proper coding practices and security testing. Web developers play a critical role in ensuring that applications remain safe and reliable.

Version control systems are essential tools in web development, enabling developers to track changes, collaborate on projects, and manage code efficiently. Git is the most widely used version control system, allowing developers to create repositories, commit changes, and merge updates from multiple contributors. GitHub, GitLab, and Bitbucket provide cloud-based hosting services for Git repositories, facilitating team collaboration and project management. By using version control, developers can maintain a history of code changes, revert to previous versions when necessary, and work collaboratively on complex web development projects.

Deployment and hosting are the final steps in bringing a web application online. Once development is complete, websites and applications must be deployed to a web server to make them accessible to users. Web hosting services such as AWS, Google Cloud, and DigitalOcean provide cloud infrastructure for hosting applications, while platforms like Netlify and Vercel offer simplified deployment for static websites and front-end applications. Continuous Integration and Continuous Deployment (CI/CD) pipelines automate the process of testing and deploying code updates, ensuring that web applications remain functional and up-to-date. Understanding the deployment process allows developers to launch web applications efficiently and manage them in a live production environment.

Web development is an exciting and dynamic field that combines creativity with technical skills to build the websites and applications that power the internet. By learning the fundamentals of front-end and back-end development, working with databases and APIs, implementing security measures, and using version control and deployment tools, developers can create high-quality web experiences. As web technologies continue to evolve, staying up to date with new frameworks, best practices, and industry trends ensures that web developers remain competitive and capable of building innovative and scalable applications.

Exploring Automation and Scripting with Python

Automation and scripting are essential skills in the IT field, helping professionals reduce repetitive tasks, increase efficiency, and minimize human error. Python has become one of the most popular programming languages for automation due to its simplicity, readability, and extensive libraries. Whether automating system administration tasks, managing network configurations, processing large datasets, or integrating different software tools, Python provides a powerful and flexible platform for scripting. Understanding how to leverage Python for automation allows IT professionals to streamline workflows and optimize various processes across industries.

Python's ease of use makes it an ideal choice for automation. Its syntax is straightforward and resembles natural language, making it accessible to beginners while offering advanced features for experienced developers. Unlike traditional programming languages that require complex syntax and compilation steps, Python scripts can be written and executed directly without additional setup. This feature makes Python an excellent tool for quick scripting tasks, enabling IT professionals to automate daily operations without extensive programming knowledge.

One of the most common areas where Python is used for automation is system administration. IT administrators often need to perform routine tasks such as managing files, monitoring system performance, updating software, and handling log files. Python's built-in modules, such as os and shutil, allow users to interact with the operating system, modify directories, and automate file operations. With just a few lines of code, a script can rename multiple files, clean up temporary directories, or generate system reports. By automating these repetitive tasks, system administrators can focus on more strategic IT initiatives while reducing the risk of manual errors.

Python is also widely used in networking automation, enabling IT professionals to configure network devices, monitor traffic, and manage security policies. The paramiko library allows scripts to establish SSH connections to remote devices, execute commands, and retrieve system information. Similarly, the netmiko library simplifies interactions with network routers and switches, making it easy to automate configuration changes across multiple devices. Automating network tasks with Python reduces the time required for manual configurations, ensures consistency across network infrastructure, and minimizes downtime caused by human mistakes.

In cybersecurity, Python plays a crucial role in automating security analysis, penetration testing, and threat detection. Security professionals use Python scripts to scan networks for vulnerabilities, analyze logs for suspicious activity, and test web applications for weaknesses. The Scapy library allows for network packet manipulation, enabling security researchers to craft custom network traffic and analyze communication protocols. Python can also be used to automate password audits, generate cryptographic hashes, and interact with APIs from security tools such as VirusTotal and Shodan. By integrating automation into cybersecurity workflows, analysts can detect and respond to threats more efficiently.

Data processing and automation are other key applications of Python scripting. Businesses generate large volumes of data that require cleaning, transformation, and analysis. Python's pandas library simplifies data manipulation, allowing users to automate the extraction, filtering, and aggregation of datasets. Organizations use Python scripts to pull data from multiple sources, clean inconsistencies, and generate reports in real time. Automating data processing tasks reduces manual labor, improves accuracy, and enables businesses to make informed decisions based on structured insights.

Python also excels at automating repetitive tasks related to web scraping and API interactions. Web scraping involves extracting data from websites, and Python's BeautifulSoup and Scrapy libraries make it easy to navigate HTML structures, retrieve specific information, and store data in structured formats. Businesses use web scraping to monitor competitor pricing, collect customer reviews, and analyze market trends. Additionally, Python simplifies API automation through libraries like requests, which allow scripts to send HTTP requests, retrieve responses, and interact with cloud services, databases, and web applications. Automating API interactions helps developers integrate different platforms and services seamlessly.

Automating office tasks is another valuable application of Python scripting. Many professionals spend significant time working with spreadsheets, emails, and PDFs. Python's openpyxl and pandas libraries enable scripts to manipulate Excel files, update financial records, and generate reports automatically. The smtplib and email modules allow Python scripts to send automated email notifications, schedule messages, and process incoming emails. The PyPDF2 library can extract text from PDF files, merge documents, and generate reports from scanned documents. Automating these office tasks enhances productivity and reduces the need for repetitive manual work.

Web automation is another powerful capability of Python, allowing users to automate browser interactions, fill out online forms, and perform repetitive web-based tasks. The Selenium library enables scripts to simulate user interactions with web pages, navigate through websites, and extract data dynamically. Companies use Selenium automation for testing web applications, verifying website functionality, and automating routine online transactions. By reducing manual effort in browser-based workflows, Python scripting helps businesses streamline their online operations.

Scheduling and task automation are essential for IT operations, and Python provides several tools for scheduling automated jobs. The schedule library allows users to run scripts at specific intervals, automating daily reports, database backups, or system maintenance tasks. The cron scheduler in Linux and Task Scheduler in Windows can execute Python scripts at predefined times, ensuring that critical processes run without human intervention. Automating task scheduling reduces operational overhead and improves system reliability by ensuring essential jobs are completed on time.

Logging and monitoring automation are also critical areas where Python excels. IT administrators and developers use Python scripts to analyze log files, detect system errors, and generate alerts based on predefined conditions. The logging module in Python provides a flexible way to track events, record system activities, and create error logs for debugging. Automated monitoring scripts can integrate with cloud-based monitoring services such as Prometheus, Grafana, and AWS CloudWatch to provide real-time insights into system performance and application health. By automating log analysis and monitoring, IT teams can identify issues early and prevent system failures.

Python's versatility in automation extends to artificial intelligence and machine learning, where scripts automate data preprocessing, model training, and predictive analysis. Libraries such as TensorFlow and scikit-learn enable developers to build AI-powered automation solutions that analyze trends, detect anomalies, and make intelligent predictions. Businesses use Python automation in AI-driven chatbots, recommendation engines, and fraud detection systems. Integrating AI with automation enhances efficiency and decision-making across various industries.

Python's rich ecosystem of libraries, ease of use, and cross-platform compatibility make it an ideal choice for automation and scripting in IT. By mastering Python scripting, IT professionals can optimize workflows, improve efficiency, and reduce manual intervention across various domains. Automation not only saves time but also enhances accuracy, security, and scalability in IT operations. Learning to leverage Python for automation opens doors to numerous career opportunities in system administration, cybersecurity, data science, and DevOps, making it one of the most valuable skills in modern IT environments.

Getting Familiar with IT Ticketing Systems

IT ticketing systems are essential tools used in businesses and organizations to track, manage, and resolve technical issues and service requests efficiently. These systems play a crucial role in IT support and service management by ensuring that problems are addressed in a structured manner. Whether handling hardware malfunctions, software troubleshooting, network outages, or user account issues, IT ticketing systems help IT teams organize their workload, prioritize tasks, and provide timely resolutions. Understanding how these systems work is essential for IT professionals, as ticketing systems are a standard feature in IT support, help desk operations, and enterprise IT service management (ITSM).

A ticketing system functions as a centralized platform where users can submit requests for technical assistance. When an issue arises, a user submits a ticket describing the problem, which is then assigned to an IT support technician or team. Each ticket contains detailed information, including the issue description, category, priority level, affected systems, and status. IT teams use the system to track the progress of the request, document troubleshooting steps, and communicate with the user until the issue is resolved. This structured approach ensures that all reported problems are addressed systematically, preventing issues from being overlooked or lost in communication.

One of the key benefits of an IT ticketing system is the ability to prioritize and categorize issues based on their urgency and impact. Not all IT problems have the same level of severity; some may require immediate attention, while others can be resolved at a later time. High-priority issues, such as network failures, server crashes, or security breaches, typically require urgent intervention, as they can disrupt business operations. Lower-priority requests, such as software installations or minor performance issues, may be scheduled for later resolution. Categorizing tickets allows IT teams to allocate resources effectively and ensure that critical incidents are handled promptly.

Most IT ticketing systems follow a lifecycle process that includes ticket creation, assignment, investigation, resolution, and closure. The process begins when a user submits a request, either through a self-service portal, email, or phone call. Once the ticket is logged, it is assigned to a technician based on expertise, availability, and workload. The technician investigates the issue by gathering relevant information, analyzing system logs, and performing necessary troubleshooting steps. If needed, the ticket may be escalated to a higher-tier support team for further analysis. After resolving the issue, the technician updates the ticket with the solution details and closes it, ensuring that the user is informed of the resolution.

Modern IT ticketing systems integrate automation features that improve efficiency and streamline support workflows. Automated ticket routing assigns requests to the appropriate team or technician based on predefined rules. Self-service knowledge bases allow users to find solutions to common problems without submitting a ticket, reducing the workload for IT support teams. Artificial intelligence and machine learning capabilities in advanced ticketing systems help predict recurring issues, suggest resolutions, and analyze trends to improve IT service delivery. Automation minimizes manual intervention, speeds up response times, and enhances overall user satisfaction.

IT ticketing systems also provide valuable insights through reporting and analytics. IT managers use ticketing system reports to assess performance metrics such as response time, resolution time, and ticket backlog. Analyzing these metrics helps identify trends, recurring issues, and areas for improvement. For example, if multiple users report the same issue, it may indicate an underlying system problem that requires a permanent fix. Data-driven insights allow IT teams to implement proactive measures, reduce downtime, and enhance the quality of support services. Regular review of ticketing system reports ensures continuous improvement in IT operations.

Several IT ticketing system platforms are widely used in businesses and organizations. Popular solutions include ServiceNow, Jira Service Management, Zendesk, Freshservice, and ManageEngine ServiceDesk Plus. Each platform offers a range of features, including multi-channel support, automation workflows, asset management, and integration with other IT tools. Organizations choose a ticketing system based on their specific needs, budget, and IT infrastructure. While some businesses require comprehensive ITSM solutions with advanced automation, others may prefer lightweight systems that focus solely on basic ticket tracking and resolution.

The implementation of IT ticketing systems follows industry best practices to ensure effectiveness. One of the key principles is clear communication between IT teams and end users. When users submit tickets, they should provide detailed descriptions, including error messages, affected systems, and steps taken before the issue occurred. IT technicians must also communicate effectively by updating ticket statuses, providing clear troubleshooting instructions, and notifying users when issues are resolved. Transparent communication reduces confusion, sets accurate expectations, and improves user satisfaction with IT support services.

Standardizing ticket handling procedures ensures consistency and efficiency in IT support. Organizations establish service level agreements (SLAs) that define response and resolution times based on ticket priority. For example, critical system failures may require resolution within a few hours, while non-urgent requests may have longer response windows. Adhering to SLAs helps IT teams manage workloads, maintain accountability, and ensure that users receive timely assistance. Training IT support staff on ticketing system best practices, documentation standards, and customer service skills further enhances the effectiveness of IT service management.

Collaboration is another important aspect of IT ticketing systems. Complex issues often require input from multiple teams, including network engineers, system administrators, and software developers. Ticketing systems facilitate collaboration by allowing technicians to share notes, escalate requests, and track ongoing investigations. Integration with communication tools such as Microsoft Teams, Slack, and email notifications ensures that IT teams stay informed and work together efficiently. By promoting teamwork, IT ticketing systems enable faster problem resolution and improve the overall support experience for users.

Security and data protection are essential considerations when using IT ticketing systems. Support requests often contain sensitive information, such as user credentials, system configurations, and security incidents. IT teams must implement access controls to ensure that only authorized personnel can view and manage tickets. Role-based access permissions restrict users from accessing information unrelated to their responsibilities. Additionally, encrypting ticket data and maintaining audit logs help protect against unauthorized access and ensure compliance with data security regulations. Proper security measures safeguard both user privacy and the integrity of IT support operations.

Learning how to navigate and use an IT ticketing system is an essential skill for IT professionals working in help desk support, system administration, and IT service management. Familiarity with ticketing platforms, troubleshooting workflows, and best practices enhances efficiency and ensures high-quality technical support. By leveraging automation, collaboration, and data-driven insights, IT teams can improve service delivery, reduce downtime, and provide a seamless user experience. Organizations that implement well-structured ticketing systems benefit from improved issue resolution, better resource management, and enhanced IT service reliability.

The Importance of Soft Skills in IT

While technical skills are crucial in the IT industry, soft skills play an equally important role in ensuring professional success. Many IT professionals focus primarily on developing expertise in programming, networking, cybersecurity, or system administration. However, the ability to communicate effectively, collaborate with teams, manage time efficiently, and adapt to changes is essential for career growth and workplace efficiency. The IT field is no longer just about working with computers and code; it also requires strong interpersonal and problem-solving abilities to navigate complex challenges and work effectively with colleagues, clients, and stakeholders.

Communication is one of the most valuable soft skills in IT. IT professionals frequently interact with team members, clients, and non-technical users who rely on their expertise to resolve technical issues and implement solutions. Clear communication ensures that technical concepts are conveyed in a way that is understandable to different audiences. Whether writing emails, documenting processes, or explaining troubleshooting steps, IT professionals must be able to articulate information concisely and effectively. Strong communication skills are also essential in meetings, presentations, and training sessions where IT professionals must explain technical details to executives or end-users who may not have a technical background.

Problem-solving is a critical skill in IT, as professionals are constantly faced with challenges that require quick thinking and logical analysis. Whether diagnosing a network issue, debugging software, or resolving a cybersecurity threat, IT professionals must approach problems methodically and find effective solutions. Strong analytical skills allow IT specialists to break down complex issues, identify root causes, and implement corrective measures efficiently. The ability to think critically and troubleshoot issues under pressure helps IT teams maintain system reliability and prevent downtime.

Collaboration and teamwork are essential in the IT industry, as most projects involve multiple stakeholders working together to achieve a common goal. Developers, network engineers, cybersecurity analysts, and IT support teams must coordinate efforts to ensure that systems function correctly and securely. Being able to work well with colleagues, listen to different perspectives, and contribute constructively to discussions leads to more successful project outcomes. Team-oriented professionals foster a positive work environment, making it easier to share knowledge, solve problems collectively, and achieve project milestones efficiently.

Adaptability is another crucial soft skill in IT, as technology is constantly evolving. IT professionals must stay up to date with the latest advancements, industry trends, and emerging threats to remain competitive in their field. Being open to learning new technologies, tools, and methodologies is essential for career growth. Adaptability also means being flexible in the workplace, as IT professionals often need to shift priorities based on business needs, respond to unexpected incidents, and work with diverse teams across different projects. Employers value professionals who can quickly adjust to changes and embrace new challenges with a proactive mindset.

Time management is a key skill that helps IT professionals stay productive and meet deadlines. IT tasks often involve multiple responsibilities, from troubleshooting technical issues and managing system updates to working on long-term projects and attending meetings. Without effective time management, tasks can pile up, leading to stress and decreased efficiency. Prioritizing tasks based on urgency and importance ensures that critical issues are addressed promptly while long-term projects remain on track. IT professionals who can manage their time effectively contribute to smoother operations and increased productivity within their teams.

Emotional intelligence plays an important role in IT, particularly in customer support and client-facing roles. IT professionals often work with users who are frustrated, confused, or experiencing technical difficulties. The ability to remain patient, listen actively, and provide empathetic support can significantly impact user satisfaction and customer relationships. Understanding emotions and responding appropriately helps build trust, improve collaboration, and create a positive work culture. Emotional intelligence also enables IT professionals to navigate workplace conflicts, handle stressful situations, and maintain professionalism in challenging circumstances.

Leadership skills are valuable in IT, even for those who are not in management positions. Leadership is not just about supervising a team; it involves taking initiative, motivating others, and setting a positive example in the workplace. IT professionals who demonstrate leadership qualities often take ownership of projects, mentor junior colleagues, and contribute innovative ideas to improve processes. Strong leadership skills can lead to career advancement opportunities, as organizations seek individuals who can inspire teams, drive innovation, and make strategic decisions.

Negotiation skills are important in IT, especially when dealing with vendors, clients, or internal stakeholders. IT professionals often need to negotiate budgets for new hardware or software, discuss project timelines, or find compromises between technical limitations and business requirements. The ability to negotiate effectively ensures that IT professionals can advocate for the best solutions while meeting business objectives. Negotiation also plays a role in resolving workplace conflicts, setting realistic expectations, and securing necessary resources for IT projects.

Customer service skills are essential for IT professionals who provide technical support, whether internally within a company or externally to clients. Providing clear instructions, maintaining professionalism, and ensuring a positive user experience contribute to higher satisfaction levels. A user-centric approach helps IT professionals build strong relationships with clients, improve service delivery, and enhance the reputation of their organization. IT support specialists, system administrators, and help desk technicians must be able to handle user requests with patience, clarity, and efficiency to ensure smooth IT operations.

Presentation and public speaking skills are beneficial for IT professionals who need to explain technical concepts to non-technical audiences. Whether presenting a security awareness training session, demonstrating a new software feature, or reporting on system performance to management, the ability to communicate ideas clearly and confidently is valuable. Many IT professionals hesitate when it comes to public speaking, but improving this skill can enhance career opportunities and help convey technical information more effectively.

Creativity is often overlooked in IT but is an important skill for problem-solving, innovation, and improving workflows. IT professionals frequently encounter unique challenges that require out-of-the-box thinking to develop effective solutions. Whether designing user-friendly software interfaces, optimizing system performance, or automating repetitive tasks, creativity allows IT professionals to find better ways to achieve their goals. Innovation is a driving force in technology, and those who think creatively can contribute to the development of new tools, applications, and security measures that improve the industry as a whole.

Work ethic and professionalism are essential traits that employers look for in IT professionals. Being reliable, meeting deadlines, taking responsibility for mistakes, and continuously striving to improve skills are qualities that contribute to long-term success. IT professionals who demonstrate commitment and dedication to their work earn the trust and respect of colleagues, clients, and management. A strong work ethic leads to greater career growth opportunities and establishes a reputation as a dependable and competent professional in the field.

The combination of technical expertise and soft skills makes IT professionals more effective in their roles. While knowing how to configure servers, write code, or secure networks is important, the ability to communicate, collaborate, adapt, and solve problems efficiently is equally critical. Soft skills enhance career prospects, improve workplace relationships, and contribute to the overall success of IT teams. Professionals who invest time in developing both technical and interpersonal skills position themselves for greater opportunities and long-term success in the ever-evolving IT industry.

Writing an IT-Focused Resume with No Experience

Breaking into the IT industry without prior experience may seem challenging, but a well-crafted resume can significantly improve the chances of landing an entry-level job. Many companies are open to hiring candidates with little or no direct experience as long as they demonstrate a strong willingness to learn, relevant technical skills, and a proactive approach to professional growth. An IT-focused resume must highlight transferable skills, educational background, certifications, personal projects, and any relevant training that showcases a candidate's ability to perform in a technical role. Even without professional experience, presenting information strategically can make a resume stand out to recruiters and hiring managers.

The first step in writing an effective IT resume is choosing the right format. A functional or skills-based resume is ideal for candidates without experience, as it emphasizes skills and knowledge rather than work history. Unlike a traditional chronological resume, which focuses on past job roles, a skills-based resume organizes information around technical abilities, education, and personal projects. This format ensures that hiring managers see the most relevant qualifications upfront, rather than focusing on the lack of formal work experience.

A well-structured resume begins with a strong summary statement. This section provides a brief overview of the candidate's skills, career aspirations, and enthusiasm for the IT field. A compelling summary should be concise and tailored to the specific job being applied for. Instead of stating a lack of experience, the focus should be on highlighting technical knowledge, problem-solving skills, and a commitment to continuous learning. For example, a resume summary might emphasize familiarity with programming languages, hands-on experience with networking concepts, or a recent IT certification that demonstrates foundational knowledge.

The skills section of the resume is one of the most important areas for candidates without experience. This section should list technical abilities relevant to the desired IT role, such as programming languages, operating systems, networking, databases, and cybersecurity principles. It is essential to include both hard skills, such as proficiency in Python, Linux, or cloud computing, and soft skills, such as problem-solving, adaptability, and teamwork. Since many entry-level IT jobs require a mix of technical and interpersonal abilities, showcasing both types of skills provides a balanced presentation of the candidate's qualifications.

Education plays a crucial role in an IT-focused resume for beginners. Candidates should list their highest level of education, including degrees, diplomas, or relevant coursework. If currently enrolled in an IT-related program, mentioning ongoing studies shows a commitment to learning. Those without formal IT education can highlight self-study efforts, online courses, or bootcamps that have provided valuable technical knowledge. Many employers recognize alternative education paths, especially in IT, where practical skills often outweigh traditional degrees. Listing completed courses from platforms such as Coursera, Udemy, or LinkedIn Learning can demonstrate self-motivation and initiative.

Certifications are a powerful addition to an IT resume, especially for candidates without experience. Industry-recognized certifications validate technical knowledge and show employers that the candidate has taken steps to acquire relevant skills. Entry-level certifications such as CompTIA A+, CompTIA Network+, and Google IT Support Professional Certificate are excellent choices for those looking to establish foundational IT knowledge. Other certifications, such as AWS Certified Cloud Practitioner or Microsoft Azure Fundamentals, can be beneficial for those interested in cloud computing. Including certifications in the resume provides credibility and makes the candidate more competitive in the job market.

Personal projects are one of the best ways to demonstrate practical IT skills on a resume. Many entry-level IT professionals gain hands-on experience by working on independent projects, contributing to open-source software, or setting up home labs. Listing personal projects allows candidates to showcase their ability to apply technical knowledge in real-world scenarios. For example, someone interested in software development might include a portfolio website, a Python automation script, or a small web application they built. Aspiring network administrators might highlight experience configuring a virtual lab using Cisco Packet Tracer or setting up a Linux server at home. Providing details about personal projects, including technologies used and challenges overcome, helps recruiters assess the candidate's problem-solving abilities.

Internships, volunteer work, and freelance experience can also be valuable additions to an IT resume. Even if unpaid, these experiences demonstrate practical application of skills in a professional setting. Volunteering to assist with IT tasks for a local organization, helping set up a website for a community group, or troubleshooting computer issues for friends and family can be relevant to entry-level IT positions. If an internship or volunteer experience involved working with software, networks, or technical support, it should be included in the resume along with the specific contributions made. Freelancing on platforms like Upwork or Fiverr, even for small projects, provides additional credibility and real-world experience that employers value.

Another effective way to enhance an IT resume is to include participation in hackathons, coding competitions, or online challenges. Many platforms, such as LeetCode, HackerRank, and TryHackMe, offer coding and cybersecurity challenges that allow candidates to test and improve their technical skills. Including rankings, achievements, or completed challenges in a resume provides tangible proof of ability and demonstrates a passion for continuous learning. Employers appreciate candidates who actively seek opportunities to improve their skills beyond traditional education.

A well-written resume should also include a section for professional development and relevant extracurricular activities. Membership in IT-related organizations, such as local tech meetups, online communities, or student coding clubs, shows engagement with the industry. Attending tech conferences, webinars, or industry networking events can also be beneficial to mention, as it demonstrates an effort to stay informed about technological trends. Employers look for candidates who show initiative and a willingness to engage with the broader IT community.

The final step in crafting a strong IT resume is ensuring clarity, professionalism, and relevance. Using a clean, well-organized layout makes the document easy to read. Each section should be clearly labeled, and bullet points should be used sparingly to highlight key achievements. Tailoring the resume to match job descriptions by using keywords from the job posting increases the chances of passing applicant tracking systems (ATS), which many companies use to screen resumes. Proofreading the resume for spelling and grammatical errors is essential to maintain a professional impression.

By focusing on technical skills, education, certifications, personal projects, and relevant experiences, candidates without formal IT experience can create a compelling resume that attracts employer attention. The key is to highlight strengths, demonstrate a commitment to learning, and showcase practical applications of knowledge. With the right approach, even those with no prior work experience in IT can create a resume that positions them as strong candidates for entry-level roles in the field.

Creating a LinkedIn Profile for IT Networking

A well-optimized LinkedIn profile is one of the most powerful tools for IT professionals looking to expand their network, showcase their skills, and increase their chances of landing job opportunities. LinkedIn is not just a social media platform; it is a professional networking space where recruiters, hiring managers, and industry experts connect. For those entering the IT field, a strong LinkedIn presence can help build credibility, establish relationships with experienced professionals, and gain insights into industry trends. Crafting a LinkedIn profile that effectively highlights skills, certifications, and projects is essential for making a positive impression and increasing visibility within the IT community.

The first step in creating an impactful LinkedIn profile is selecting a professional profile picture. A high-quality headshot with good lighting and a neutral background helps create a strong first impression. IT professionals should aim for a polished yet approachable appearance, as recruiters and potential connections often judge credibility based on profile pictures. A professional image increases the likelihood of profile views and connection requests, making it easier to network with industry professionals.

The headline is one of the most important elements of a LinkedIn profile. It appears directly under the name and serves as a quick introduction to a candidate's professional identity. Instead of simply listing "IT Enthusiast" or "Aspiring IT Professional," a more effective headline includes specific skills or career aspirations. For example, a strong headline might read "Entry-Level IT Specialist | CompTIA A+ Certified | Passionate About Cybersecurity & Networking." A well-crafted headline immediately informs visitors about the candidate's focus and expertise, making it easier for recruiters and industry professionals to identify relevant profiles.

The summary section, also known as the "About" section, is an opportunity to provide a more detailed introduction. This section should highlight technical skills, career goals, and personal motivation for entering the IT field. A compelling summary tells a story about the candidate's journey, mentioning how they developed an interest in technology, what skills they have acquired, and what roles they are pursuing. For those without direct IT experience, emphasizing certifications, self-study efforts, and hands-on projects can demonstrate dedication and passion. A well-written summary should be engaging, concise, and free of generic phrases that do not add value.

The experience section of a LinkedIn profile may seem challenging for those without formal IT jobs, but it can still be used effectively. Even if someone has not worked in IT professionally, listing relevant volunteer work, internships, freelance projects, or self-initiated tech-related activities can provide credibility. Descriptions of projects, such as setting up a home network, automating tasks with Python scripts, or troubleshooting IT issues for friends and family, help showcase practical skills. For those who have transitioned from another industry, highlighting transferable skills such as problem-solving, analytical thinking, and teamwork can add value to the experience section.

Certifications play a crucial role in an IT-focused LinkedIn profile. Many recruiters search for candidates based on certifications, making it important to list them in a dedicated section. Certifications such as CompTIA A+, Network+, Security+, Cisco's CCNA, AWS Certified Cloud Practitioner, and Microsoft Azure Fundamentals help establish technical credibility. Including relevant certifications increases the likelihood of appearing in recruiter searches and signals commitment to professional development. Additionally, linking to certification badges from platforms like Credly enhances authenticity and visibility.

The skills section allows IT professionals to list their technical competencies, which can include programming languages, networking concepts, cybersecurity tools, cloud platforms, and troubleshooting expertise. It is important to prioritize skills that align with career goals and desired job roles. LinkedIn allows connections to endorse skills, and having multiple endorsements increases credibility. Actively requesting endorsements from colleagues, classmates, or mentors can help build a stronger professional profile.

Engagement on LinkedIn plays a vital role in expanding professional networks and establishing credibility. IT professionals should regularly share content, participate in discussions, and comment on industry-related posts. Posting about recent achievements, completed projects, or insights gained from studying IT topics can demonstrate expertise and enthusiasm for the field. Engaging with thought leaders, following IT-related groups, and contributing to discussions on technology trends increase visibility and networking opportunities. A well-maintained and active LinkedIn presence signals to recruiters that a candidate is serious about their professional growth.

The recommendations section adds further validation to a LinkedIn profile. A strong recommendation from a mentor, instructor, or colleague provides additional credibility. Requesting recommendations from individuals who can speak about technical skills, problem-solving abilities, and work ethic strengthens the profile. Personalized recommendations that highlight specific accomplishments or contributions are more valuable than generic endorsements.

LinkedIn allows users to feature projects, articles, and multimedia content in the "Featured" section. For IT professionals, showcasing personal projects, GitHub repositories, blog posts, or video tutorials can demonstrate hands-on skills. Including links to coding projects, home lab configurations, cybersecurity challenges, or cloud deployments provides concrete examples of technical abilities. A portfolio of work helps differentiate candidates from others who may only list skills without demonstrating practical applications.

Networking on LinkedIn involves more than just creating a profile; it requires actively building connections with industry professionals. Sending personalized connection requests to IT professionals, recruiters, and individuals working in target companies increases networking opportunities. When sending requests, including a brief message explaining mutual interests or career aspirations makes the interaction more meaningful. Connecting with individuals in entry-level IT roles can provide valuable insights into job opportunities and career growth strategies. Engaging in meaningful conversations with IT professionals fosters long-term relationships and mentorship opportunities.

Job searching on LinkedIn is another significant advantage of maintaining a strong profile. The platform offers job postings specifically tailored to IT professionals, and many companies actively use LinkedIn to recruit candidates. Setting up job alerts, following company pages, and applying directly through LinkedIn increases exposure to potential employers. Some job postings allow applicants to apply using their LinkedIn profile, making it essential to keep the profile updated and optimized. Engaging with recruiters and hiring managers by commenting on job postings or sending follow-up messages can improve the chances of securing interviews.

Joining LinkedIn groups related to IT provides additional networking and learning opportunities. Groups focused on networking, cybersecurity, cloud computing, and programming offer valuable discussions, job postings, and industry updates. Participating in group conversations, asking technical questions, and sharing experiences help build a presence within the IT community. Many recruiters and employers actively search for candidates in industry-specific groups, making group participation an effective way to increase visibility.

Consistency in maintaining a LinkedIn profile is key to long-term success. Regularly updating certifications, adding new skills, and sharing industry insights keep the profile fresh and relevant. As IT professionals gain experience, updating job roles, achievements, and projects ensures that the profile reflects current expertise. Staying engaged with the platform and continuously expanding connections strengthens professional opportunities and career growth.

A well-optimized LinkedIn profile is an essential tool for IT networking, career advancement, and job searching. By strategically highlighting skills, certifications, projects, and professional connections, IT professionals can increase their visibility, attract recruiters, and establish credibility in the industry. Actively engaging with the IT community and continuously improving the profile ensures long-term success in building a strong professional presence.

Finding and Applying for Entry-Level IT Jobs

Breaking into the IT industry can be challenging, especially for those without prior experience. However, the demand for IT professionals continues to grow, and many companies are willing to hire entry-level candidates who demonstrate strong technical skills, problem-solving abilities, and a willingness to learn. Finding and applying for entry-level IT jobs requires a strategic approach, from identifying the right job opportunities to crafting a compelling application that captures the attention of recruiters. By leveraging job boards, networking platforms, and personal projects, aspiring IT professionals can increase their chances of securing their first job in the industry.

The first step in the job search process is understanding which entry-level IT roles align with personal skills and career goals. Common entry-level positions include IT support specialist, help desk technician, junior network administrator, junior software developer, cybersecurity analyst trainee, and technical support engineer. Each of these roles requires different skill sets, so it is important to assess strengths and interests before applying. IT support and help desk roles focus on troubleshooting and assisting users with technical issues, while network administrators manage and configure network infrastructure. Junior developers work on programming tasks, and cybersecurity analysts help protect systems from threats. Identifying a preferred IT path helps narrow down job search efforts and ensures that applications are targeted toward relevant roles.

Job boards are one of the most effective ways to find entry-level IT job postings. Websites such as Indeed, LinkedIn Jobs, Glassdoor, and ZipRecruiter list thousands of IT job openings, many of which are suitable for beginners. When searching for jobs, using keywords such as "entry-level IT," "junior IT technician," "help desk," or "IT support specialist" helps refine search results. Many job boards allow users to set up email alerts, ensuring that new job postings matching specific criteria are delivered directly to their inbox. Staying updated on job listings increases the chances of applying early, which can be an advantage in competitive hiring processes.

LinkedIn is an invaluable resource for job seekers, offering not only job postings but also networking opportunities. Many recruiters actively search for candidates on LinkedIn, making it essential to have a well-optimized profile that highlights skills, certifications, and relevant experience. Following IT companies, engaging with industry professionals, and joining IT-related groups can lead to job leads and referrals. Connecting with recruiters and sending personalized messages expressing interest in entry-level IT positions can also help candidates gain visibility. Employers appreciate candidates who take the initiative to reach out and express enthusiasm for their open roles.

Building a strong resume tailored for IT positions is crucial for standing out in the job application process. Even without direct IT experience, showcasing relevant skills, certifications, personal projects, and volunteer work can make a resume compelling. Highlighting technical skills such as proficiency in operating systems, networking concepts, programming languages, and troubleshooting techniques demonstrates readiness for IT roles. Certifications such as CompTIA A+, Network+, and Google IT Support Professional Certificate validate technical knowledge and improve credibility. Personal projects, such as building a website, configuring a home network, or automating tasks with Python, showcase practical skills that hiring managers value.

A well-crafted cover letter can further enhance an application by providing insight into a candidate's passion for IT and motivation for applying to a specific role. A strong cover letter should briefly introduce the candidate, highlight relevant skills and certifications, and explain why they are interested in the position. Expressing enthusiasm for the company and demonstrating knowledge of its industry or services shows recruiters that the applicant has done their research. Since many entry-level candidates lack professional experience, a cover letter is an opportunity to explain how self-learning, coursework, or personal projects have prepared them for the role.

Internships and apprenticeships are excellent ways to gain hands-on experience and transition into full-time IT roles. Many companies offer internship programs designed for individuals with little to no experience, providing them with real-world exposure to IT tasks. While some internships are unpaid or offer lower salaries, they provide invaluable experience that can be included on a resume and LinkedIn profile. Apprenticeship programs, particularly in cybersecurity, networking, and cloud computing, offer structured training that helps candidates gain technical expertise while working on real projects. Applying for internships and apprenticeships can be a stepping stone toward securing a permanent IT position.

Freelancing and volunteer work can also provide practical IT experience that strengthens job applications. Platforms such as Upwork and Fiverr allow individuals to offer IT services, including technical support, website development, and network troubleshooting. While freelancing may not offer the same structure as a full-time job, it helps build a portfolio of work that demonstrates technical abilities. Volunteering for nonprofit organizations, community groups, or local businesses by assisting with IT-related tasks, such as setting up computer systems, troubleshooting software issues, or managing websites, provides valuable hands-on experience. These experiences can be added to a resume and serve as proof of practical knowledge.

Attending IT networking events, career fairs, and webinars increases exposure to job opportunities and allows job seekers to interact with industry professionals. Many companies participate in job fairs to recruit entry-level talent, and these events provide a chance to meet hiring managers in person. Virtual networking events and IT conferences also offer opportunities to learn about industry trends and connect with professionals who may offer job referrals. Establishing relationships with experienced IT professionals can lead to mentorship opportunities and insider job recommendations. Many IT professionals secure their first job through referrals rather than traditional job applications.

Practicing for job interviews is essential for making a strong impression on potential employers. Many IT job interviews include technical questions, problem-solving exercises, and behavioral questions to assess a candidate's ability to handle real-world scenarios. Preparing for common IT interview questions, such as troubleshooting steps for network issues, explaining differences between operating systems, or demonstrating knowledge of cybersecurity best practices, helps candidates feel confident. Mock interviews with friends, mentors, or online resources improve communication skills and reduce interview anxiety. Employers value candidates who can articulate their thought processes and demonstrate a problem-solving mindset.

Applying to multiple positions and following up with employers increases the likelihood of securing a job. Since job markets are competitive, submitting applications to a variety of roles ensures a higher chance of receiving interview invitations. Following up on applications by sending polite emails to hiring managers or recruiters demonstrates professionalism and persistence. Expressing continued interest in a position and requesting updates on application status keeps candidates on the employer's radar. Employers appreciate proactive candidates who show dedication and enthusiasm for their job search.

Breaking into the IT field requires determination, continuous learning, and a proactive job search strategy. By leveraging job boards, networking platforms, internships, freelancing, and strong application materials, candidates can improve their chances of securing their first entry-level IT job. Employers value skills, motivation, and problem-solving abilities over formal experience, making it possible for new professionals to enter the industry through self-learning, certifications, and practical projects. Taking a strategic and persistent approach to job searching helps aspiring IT professionals build a successful career in technology.

The Importance of Internships and Volunteer Work

Gaining practical experience is one of the biggest challenges for individuals entering the IT industry. Many job postings, even for entry-level positions, require some level of experience, which can make it difficult for newcomers to break into the field. Internships and volunteer work provide an excellent way to gain hands-on experience, develop technical skills, and build a professional network. While these opportunities may not always offer high salaries, they provide valuable real-world experience that enhances a resume, increases employability, and sets the foundation for a successful IT career.

Internships offer structured learning experiences that expose candidates to real-world IT environments. Unlike academic learning, which focuses on theory and concepts, internships allow individuals to apply their knowledge to actual problems faced by businesses and organizations. Interns often work alongside experienced IT professionals, gaining insights into workplace practices, troubleshooting techniques, and industry best practices. Whether assisting in network maintenance, writing code for software applications, or responding to IT support tickets, interns develop technical and problem-solving skills that cannot be fully acquired through coursework alone.

Many IT companies, ranging from large corporations to small startups, offer internship programs designed to train new talent. These programs provide structured mentorship, hands-on projects, and exposure to various aspects of IT operations. Interns may have opportunities to work with advanced technologies, collaborate on software development, or contribute to cybersecurity initiatives. Large companies often use internships as a recruitment pipeline, evaluating interns for full-time positions upon completion of the program. Even if an internship does not result in an immediate job offer, it provides a strong addition to a resume and valuable industry connections.

One of the key advantages of internships is the ability to explore different IT career paths before committing to a specific role. Many newcomers to the IT field are unsure whether they want to specialize in software development, network administration, cybersecurity, cloud computing, or another area. Internships allow individuals to gain exposure to multiple fields, helping them make informed career decisions. Some interns discover new interests during their placements, leading them to pursue specializations they had not previously considered. By experiencing different aspects of IT work, interns can refine their career goals and tailor their skill development accordingly.

Internships also help bridge the gap between academic learning and workplace expectations. Many IT roles require skills beyond technical knowledge, including teamwork, communication, and project management. Working in an IT environment teaches interns how to collaborate with colleagues, document technical procedures, and manage deadlines. Learning how to navigate workplace dynamics and handle professional responsibilities prepares individuals for full-time employment. Employers value candidates who have experience working in a structured environment, as it demonstrates an ability to adapt to the demands of a professional IT setting.

Volunteer work provides another valuable pathway for gaining IT experience, particularly for individuals who may not have access to formal internship programs. Nonprofit organizations, community groups, and small businesses often have IT needs but lack the resources to hire full-time professionals. Volunteering to assist with IT tasks, such as setting up computer networks, troubleshooting software issues, or maintaining websites, allows individuals to gain hands-on experience while contributing to a meaningful cause. Unlike internships, which may have structured programs, volunteer work often provides greater flexibility, allowing individuals to tailor their involvement based on their availability and interests.

One of the biggest benefits of volunteer work is the opportunity to take on responsibilities that might not be available in a traditional entry-level job. Many IT volunteers work independently or in small teams, handling tasks that would typically be assigned to experienced professionals. This level of responsibility provides valuable learning experiences, allowing volunteers to develop leadership, problem-solving, and decision-making skills. Managing IT projects, setting up cybersecurity measures, or optimizing software solutions for an organization demonstrates initiative and expertise, making a strong impression on future employers.

Volunteer work also serves as a networking tool, helping individuals connect with industry professionals and expand their job search opportunities. Many organizations that rely on volunteers have connections with IT companies, recruiters, or professionals who can provide job referrals or mentorship. Demonstrating commitment and technical abilities through volunteer work can lead to recommendations, contract opportunities, or even full-time job offers. Networking within nonprofit organizations, local community tech groups, or open-source projects exposes individuals to valuable industry contacts who can support their career development.

For those looking to specialize in cybersecurity, volunteering with security-focused organizations provides an excellent way to gain practical experience. Ethical hacking groups, cybersecurity nonprofits, and online security challenges offer hands-on experience with penetration testing, vulnerability assessments, and security analysis. Participating in capture-the-flag competitions, security audits, or digital forensics investigations as a volunteer enhances technical skills and demonstrates expertise in the field. Employers in the cybersecurity industry highly value hands-on experience, making volunteer work a great way to build a competitive resume.

Students and career changers can also benefit from contributing to open-source projects as a form of volunteer work. Many technology companies, developers, and software communities maintain open-source projects that welcome contributions from individuals of all skill levels. Working on open-source projects provides practical coding experience, exposes contributors to collaborative software development practices, and allows them to showcase their work publicly. Platforms like GitHub and GitLab serve as excellent spaces for IT professionals to share their projects, collaborate with others, and build a portfolio that demonstrates real-world coding and problem-solving abilities.

Adding internship and volunteer experience to a resume helps candidates stand out in the competitive IT job market. Many hiring managers prioritize practical experience over formal education, and internships or volunteer work demonstrate a candidate's ability to apply technical skills in real-world scenarios. Including details about projects completed, technologies used, and problem-solving contributions provides concrete examples of technical competence. Employers appreciate candidates who take initiative, gain experience through nontraditional routes, and demonstrate a commitment to professional development.

Internships and volunteer work also provide confidence and self-assurance when applying for IT jobs. Many candidates hesitate to apply for roles due to a lack of direct work experience, but hands-on involvement in IT projects helps build confidence in technical abilities. Having experience troubleshooting real problems, collaborating with teams, and working on live systems prepares candidates for the challenges of a full-time IT role. Confidence gained through practical experience enhances performance in job interviews, where candidates must explain their technical knowledge and problem-solving approach.

While formal education and certifications are valuable, they are not always enough to secure a job in IT. Employers seek candidates who have demonstrated their skills in real-world situations, making internships and volunteer work essential for building a strong professional foundation. By taking advantage of these opportunities, aspiring IT professionals can gain experience, build a portfolio of work, expand their professional network, and improve their chances of securing a full-time job. Those who actively seek out internships and volunteer work position themselves for greater career success and long-term growth in the IT industry.

Building a Simple IT Portfolio

Creating an IT portfolio is one of the most effective ways to showcase technical skills, projects, and problem-solving abilities to potential employers. While a resume provides an overview of qualifications, a portfolio demonstrates practical experience through tangible examples of work. Many entry-level IT professionals struggle to stand out in the competitive job market, especially without formal experience. A well-organized portfolio provides a solution by offering proof of technical expertise, self-initiated learning, and a commitment to continuous improvement. Whether applying for jobs in IT support, software development, networking, or cybersecurity, a strong portfolio can significantly improve job prospects.

The first step in building an IT portfolio is selecting a platform to host it. A personal website is an excellent option, as it allows complete customization and provides a professional online presence. Platforms like GitHub Pages, Netlify, and WordPress offer free hosting solutions for those starting out. For developers, GitHub serves as both a portfolio and a version control system where code repositories can be shared with recruiters and potential employers. Those who specialize in networking, cybersecurity, or IT support may choose to create a simple blog or online documentation that details projects and problem-solving experiences. The goal is to have a centralized location where employers can easily review past work.

A well-structured IT portfolio should include a clear introduction, highlighting technical skills, career goals, and a brief personal background. The introduction should be concise and focus on relevant experience, certifications, and areas of expertise. A professional photo and contact information, such as an email address and LinkedIn profile, add credibility and make it easier for recruiters to connect. While personal details are important, the main focus of the portfolio should be on projects and technical demonstrations that showcase hands-on experience.

Projects are the most critical component of an IT portfolio. The projects included should demonstrate proficiency in different technical areas, such as troubleshooting, scripting, networking, system administration, or cybersecurity. Those with an interest in software development can showcase small applications, automation scripts, or contributions to open-source projects. Networking professionals can document home lab setups, network configurations, or security monitoring systems they have implemented. Cybersecurity enthusiasts may include penetration testing exercises, vulnerability assessments, or forensic investigations. Each project should be presented with a description of the problem, the technologies used, and the steps taken to complete the project.

For IT professionals who specialize in troubleshooting and support, a portfolio can include case studies of technical issues resolved. A breakdown of common problems encountered, troubleshooting steps taken, and final resolutions can demonstrate problem-solving skills. Screenshots, configuration files, and command-line outputs provide additional details that showcase technical expertise. Writing detailed documentation for each project not only enhances the portfolio but also improves technical writing skills, which are highly valued in IT roles.

A portfolio should also highlight certifications and technical training. Many IT roles require certifications as proof of knowledge in specific areas, and displaying earned certifications in the portfolio reinforces credibility. Certifications such as CompTIA A+, Network+, Security+, Cisco CCNA, AWS Cloud Practitioner, and Microsoft Azure Fundamentals demonstrate expertise in foundational IT concepts. If possible, adding digital certification badges or links to official verification pages ensures authenticity. Online courses, bootcamps, and workshops attended can also be included as part of the professional development section of the portfolio.

An effective way to make a portfolio stand out is by adding interactive elements that allow potential employers to engage with the work. Developers can host live versions of their applications, allowing visitors to test functionality in real time. Network engineers can create interactive network diagrams using tools like Cisco Packet Tracer, providing visual representations of network topologies they have designed. Cybersecurity professionals can share walkthroughs of ethical hacking challenges or security assessments, demonstrating step-by-step processes for identifying vulnerabilities and implementing fixes. Providing access to practical demonstrations makes the portfolio more engaging and memorable.

For those new to IT, starting small with beginner-level projects is perfectly acceptable. Simple projects such as setting up a virtual machine, writing a basic Python script to automate a task, or configuring a home firewall can be valuable additions to a portfolio. The key is to document the learning process, challenges encountered, and lessons gained from each project. Employers value candidates who show initiative and a willingness to learn, even if the projects are not highly complex. A well-documented beginner project can often be more impressive than an incomplete advanced project.

A blog section can enhance an IT portfolio by demonstrating thought leadership and technical communication skills. Writing articles about completed projects, industry trends, troubleshooting guides, or best practices in IT showcases expertise beyond practical work. Blog posts allow professionals to share knowledge, contribute to the IT community, and establish themselves as knowledgeable individuals in their field. Employers appreciate candidates who actively engage in self-improvement and knowledge sharing, making a blog a valuable addition to any portfolio.

A portfolio should be kept up to date as new skills are learned and additional projects are completed. Regularly adding new work ensures that the portfolio reflects current abilities and knowledge. As technology evolves, IT professionals should continue learning and experimenting with new tools, frameworks, and methodologies. Keeping a version history of projects, documenting progress, and reflecting on improvements made over time shows growth and adaptability. A regularly updated portfolio demonstrates continuous learning and keeps candidates competitive in the job market.

Professionalism is important when designing an IT portfolio. The layout should be clean, easy to navigate, and visually appealing. Using a simple and modern design ensures that the focus remains on content rather than unnecessary distractions. Grammar, spelling, and formatting should be reviewed carefully to maintain credibility. Providing downloadable resumes, direct contact forms, and links to LinkedIn profiles further improves accessibility and increases networking opportunities.

Once an IT portfolio is complete, it should be actively shared with recruiters, hiring managers, and professional networks. Adding the portfolio link to a resume, LinkedIn profile, and job applications increases visibility. Engaging with IT communities, participating in open-source projects, and contributing to forums like GitHub, Stack Overflow, or LinkedIn Groups can help attract attention from potential employers. Many job seekers have landed opportunities simply by having an impressive portfolio that demonstrates technical skills effectively.

An IT portfolio is a powerful tool that helps bridge the gap between theoretical knowledge and practical experience. By including well-documented projects, certifications, training, and interactive demonstrations, IT professionals can showcase their abilities and stand out in the competitive job market. Employers value candidates who take the initiative to build a portfolio, as it provides tangible proof of skills, work ethic, and problem-solving capabilities. Investing time in creating and maintaining a high-quality portfolio opens doors to job opportunities and career advancement in the IT industry.

Practicing for IT Job Interviews

Preparing for an IT job interview is one of the most critical steps in securing a position in the field. While having the right technical skills is essential, the ability to communicate effectively, demonstrate problem-solving abilities, and present oneself professionally can significantly impact the outcome of an interview. Many candidates make the mistake of only focusing on technical knowledge, but IT job interviews often include behavioral questions, practical exercises, and discussions about real-world scenarios. A well-rounded preparation strategy involves studying technical topics, practicing coding or troubleshooting exercises, improving communication skills, and understanding the company's expectations.

One of the first steps in preparing for an IT interview is researching the company and the role. Employers appreciate candidates who show an understanding of their business, services, and technologies. Reviewing the company's website, recent news articles, and job descriptions helps candidates tailor their responses to align with the organization's needs. Understanding the company's tech stack, preferred tools, and industry focus allows candidates to highlight relevant skills and demonstrate genuine interest in the role. Being able to discuss how personal skills and experience align with the company's goals makes a positive impression on hiring managers.

Technical preparation is a crucial aspect of IT job interviews. Depending on the role, candidates may need to demonstrate proficiency in networking, cybersecurity, programming, cloud computing, or system administration. Reviewing core concepts and practicing common technical questions is essential for building confidence. For software development roles, practicing coding problems on platforms like LeetCode, HackerRank, or CodeSignal helps improve problem-solving speed and algorithmic thinking. For networking and system administration positions, reviewing networking protocols, troubleshooting methods, and common configurations ensures readiness for practical assessments.

Many IT interviews include hands-on exercises, such as coding tests, network troubleshooting scenarios, or system administration tasks. Practicing real-world problems in a simulated environment helps candidates gain confidence in their technical abilities. Setting up a home lab using virtualization tools, practicing command-line operations, and working on personal projects provides valuable hands-on experience. Some companies may conduct live coding sessions or technical whiteboard challenges, requiring candidates to explain their thought processes while solving problems. Practicing explaining solutions out loud helps develop clear and structured communication during technical assessments.

Behavioral questions are a common part of IT interviews, as employers want to assess problem-solving skills, teamwork, and adaptability. Questions such as "Tell me about a time you solved a technical problem," "Describe a challenging project you worked on," or "How do you handle conflicts in a team?" require structured responses. The STAR method (Situation, Task, Action, Result) is an effective way to answer behavioral questions by providing context, explaining actions taken, and describing the outcome. Preparing examples from past experiences, even from personal projects or coursework, helps candidates answer behavioral questions confidently.

Soft skills play a significant role in IT job interviews. Employers look for candidates who can work well in teams, communicate effectively, and handle pressure. Practicing clear and concise explanations of technical concepts is important, especially when interviewing for roles that involve customer interactions or cross-department collaboration. IT professionals often need to explain complex topics to non-technical stakeholders, making communication skills essential. Practicing mock interviews with friends, mentors, or online resources helps refine answers and improve confidence in verbal responses.

Many IT interviews include questions about troubleshooting and problem-solving approaches. Employers want to see how candidates analyze issues, break down problems, and arrive at solutions.

Practicing troubleshooting scenarios, such as diagnosing network outages, resolving system crashes, or debugging code, helps candidates develop a logical approach to problem-solving. Structuring answers by describing the issue, listing possible causes, testing solutions, and verifying results demonstrates a methodical problem-solving mindset. Employers appreciate candidates who can think critically and remain calm under pressure.

Understanding industry trends and best practices is another important part of IT interview preparation. Employers often ask about emerging technologies, cybersecurity threats, or cloud computing trends to assess a candidate's awareness of the field. Keeping up with industry news, attending webinars, and following thought leaders in IT helps candidates stay informed. Being able to discuss relevant trends, such as DevOps practices, automation, or AI in cybersecurity, shows initiative and a commitment to continuous learning. Employers value candidates who demonstrate curiosity and a proactive approach to staying updated with technological advancements.

Practicing for remote interviews is essential, as many IT companies conduct virtual interviews. Ensuring a stable internet connection, testing video conferencing software, and using a professional background create a good impression. Speaking clearly, maintaining eye contact, and minimizing distractions help improve virtual interview presence. Preparing notes with key talking points, such as technical strengths, project experiences, and company-specific research, allows candidates to reference important details without losing focus. Being comfortable with remote interview etiquette enhances confidence and professionalism.

Time management and preparation before the interview contribute to success. Reviewing the interview schedule, setting reminders, and organizing necessary materials ensures a smooth interview process. Preparing a list of thoughtful questions to ask the interviewer demonstrates engagement and interest in the role. Questions about team structure, career growth opportunities, and company culture help candidates evaluate whether the job aligns with their career goals. Employers appreciate candidates who ask insightful questions, as it shows initiative and a genuine investment in the position.

Receiving and responding to feedback is an important part of the interview process. If a candidate is unsuccessful, requesting feedback from the interviewer can provide valuable insights for improvement. Constructive feedback helps identify areas that need further development, whether in technical skills, communication, or problem-solving. Learning from past interviews and refining responses based on feedback improves performance in future interviews. Candidates who continuously refine their approach increase their chances of securing an IT position.

Confidence plays a key role in IT job interviews. Many candidates have the necessary skills but struggle with self-doubt or imposter syndrome. Practicing interview scenarios, preparing structured answers, and reinforcing technical knowledge help build confidence. Reminding oneself of achievements, completed projects, and learning progress reinforces a positive mindset. Approaching interviews with a growth-oriented attitude, rather than focusing solely on outcomes, reduces anxiety and improves overall performance. Employers recognize and appreciate candidates who are self-assured, enthusiastic, and eager to contribute to their teams.

Thorough preparation for IT job interviews involves a combination of technical study, problem-solving practice, communication skills development, and industry awareness. By practicing structured responses, engaging in hands-on exercises, and improving confidence in answering questions, candidates can increase their chances of success. Employers seek candidates who not only possess technical expertise but also demonstrate adaptability, teamwork, and problem-solving abilities. A well-prepared candidate stands out in interviews and is more likely to secure opportunities in the competitive IT job market.

Understanding IT Job Roles and Their Differences

The IT industry offers a wide range of job roles, each requiring specific skills and knowledge. Understanding the differences between these roles helps individuals choose the right career path based on their interests, strengths, and professional goals. While some IT positions focus on software development and programming, others specialize in networking, cybersecurity, system administration, data analysis, or cloud computing. Knowing the responsibilities and expectations of each role is essential for anyone entering the IT field, as it allows them to develop the necessary skills and prepare effectively for job opportunities.

One of the most common entry-level roles in IT is the IT support specialist or help desk technician. These professionals provide technical assistance to end users, troubleshooting hardware and software issues. They help install applications, configure devices, and resolve connectivity problems. IT support specialists are often the first point of contact for users experiencing technical difficulties, making strong communication and problem-solving skills essential. This role provides valuable experience for those looking to transition into more specialized IT careers, such as system administration, networking, or cybersecurity.

System administrators are responsible for managing and maintaining an organization's IT infrastructure. They oversee servers, operating systems, and enterprise applications, ensuring that systems remain operational and secure. Their tasks include configuring user accounts, managing backups, and monitoring system performance. System administrators work closely with IT support teams to resolve complex issues and implement security policies. Knowledge of Linux, Windows Server, virtualization, and automation tools such as PowerShell or Bash scripting is highly beneficial in this role.

Network administrators focus on designing, implementing, and maintaining computer networks. They configure routers, switches, and firewalls to ensure stable and secure connectivity within an organization. Network administrators also troubleshoot network issues, optimize performance, and enforce security measures to protect data transmission. Certifications such as CompTIA Network+ or Cisco's CCNA are valuable for professionals entering this field. As networks become more complex, expertise in cloud networking, wireless technology, and virtual private networks (VPNs) is increasingly important.

Cybersecurity analysts play a crucial role in protecting organizations from cyber threats. They monitor network activity for suspicious behavior, investigate security incidents, and implement measures to prevent data breaches. Cybersecurity analysts use tools such as firewalls, intrusion detection systems (IDS), and encryption technologies to safeguard information. They also conduct vulnerability assessments and penetration testing to identify weaknesses in security defenses. Certifications such as CompTIA Security+, Certified Ethical Hacker (CEH), and CISSP help professionals build credibility in this field.

Software developers and programmers focus on designing and building applications, websites, and software solutions. They write code using programming languages such as Python, Java, C++, JavaScript, and SQL. Software developers collaborate with designers, project managers, and testers to create functional and efficient applications. Web developers specialize in front-end, back-end, or full-stack development, working with frameworks such as React, Angular, or Django. Mobile app developers focus on building applications for iOS and Android platforms. Software engineering is a broad field that includes roles in artificial intelligence, game development, and embedded systems programming.

Database administrators (DBAs) manage and maintain databases used to store, organize, and retrieve data. They ensure that databases are secure, optimized for performance, and backed up regularly. Database administrators work with relational database management systems (RDBMS) such as MySQL, PostgreSQL, Microsoft SQL Server, and Oracle. They write SQL queries, configure access permissions, and implement disaster recovery strategies. Data integrity and security are key responsibilities in this role, making knowledge of encryption techniques and compliance regulations essential.

Cloud engineers specialize in designing and managing cloud-based infrastructure and services. They work with cloud platforms such as Amazon Web Services (AWS), Microsoft Azure, and Google Cloud to deploy and maintain applications in the cloud. Cloud engineers configure virtual machines, manage storage solutions, and optimize cloud security. As more businesses migrate to cloud environments, expertise in cloud architecture, serverless computing, and containerization using Docker and Kubernetes is increasingly in demand. Certifications such as AWS Certified Solutions Architect or Microsoft Certified: Azure Administrator help professionals stand out in this field.

DevOps engineers bridge the gap between development and operations teams, focusing on automation, continuous integration, and deployment (CI/CD). They streamline software development and deployment processes by implementing automation tools and practices. DevOps engineers work with scripting languages, cloud platforms, and containerization technologies to improve software delivery pipelines. They also monitor application performance and collaborate with developers to enhance system reliability. Knowledge of tools such as Jenkins, Terraform, Ansible, and Kubernetes is essential for professionals in this role.

IT project managers oversee the planning, execution, and completion of IT projects within an organization. They coordinate teams, manage resources, and ensure that projects are delivered on time and within budget. IT project managers need strong leadership and organizational skills, as well as knowledge of project management methodologies such as Agile and Scrum. They often work with software development, network infrastructure, or cybersecurity teams to align IT projects with business objectives. Certifications such as PMP (Project Management Professional) and Certified Scrum Master (CSM) are valuable for professionals pursuing this career path.

Data analysts and data scientists specialize in analyzing and interpreting large datasets to generate insights that drive business decisions. Data analysts use tools such as SQL, Excel, and visualization software like Tableau or Power BI to create reports and dashboards. Data scientists take analysis further by using machine learning algorithms and statistical modeling to predict trends and automate decision-making. They work with programming languages such as Python and R, as well as frameworks like TensorFlow and Scikit-learn. The growing importance of big data has increased demand for professionals with expertise in data management, analytics, and artificial intelligence.

Ethical hackers and penetration testers focus on testing an organization's security defenses by simulating cyberattacks. They use hacking techniques to identify vulnerabilities in systems, networks, and applications before malicious attackers can exploit them. Ethical hackers perform security audits, conduct penetration testing exercises, and recommend security improvements. Knowledge of scripting, exploit development, and penetration testing tools such as Metasploit, Burp Suite, and Kali Linux is essential in this field. Certifications like Offensive Security Certified Professional (OSCP) and Certified Ethical Hacker (CEH) validate skills in ethical hacking and security assessment.

Technical support engineers assist customers and employees with technical issues related to software, hardware, and IT services. They troubleshoot problems, provide solutions, and escalate complex issues to specialized teams. Technical support roles may be remote or in-person, and they require excellent problem-solving and communication skills. Some professionals in this field specialize in enterprise IT support, helping businesses maintain their internal systems, while others focus on customer-facing support for software products.

Each IT job role requires a unique set of skills and expertise, and professionals often transition between roles as they gain experience and specialize in different areas. Understanding these job roles helps individuals identify the career paths that align with their interests and goals. By developing relevant skills, obtaining certifications, and gaining hands-on experience, aspiring IT professionals can successfully enter the field and advance in their chosen careers.

How to Get Your First Freelance IT Gig

Freelancing in IT provides an excellent opportunity to gain experience, earn income, and build a professional reputation. For those new to the industry, securing the first freelance gig can be challenging, but with the right approach, it is possible to land projects even without an extensive portfolio. Many businesses and individuals require IT services, such as website development, software troubleshooting, cybersecurity assessments, or system administration, and are willing to hire freelancers for these tasks. Finding the first freelance job involves identifying skills, creating an online presence, networking, and using freelance platforms to connect with clients.

The first step in getting a freelance IT gig is identifying the specific skills and services to offer. IT is a broad field, and clients look for specialists in areas such as technical support, network configuration, cloud computing, web development, cybersecurity, or automation. Beginners should focus on a niche that aligns with their expertise and learning path. Offering targeted services, such as setting up WordPress websites, fixing computer issues, configuring routers, or automating Excel tasks with Python, helps attract potential clients looking for specific solutions. Starting with small, well-defined services makes it easier to gain experience and build confidence.

Building a strong online presence is crucial for attracting freelance opportunities. A professional LinkedIn profile that highlights IT skills, certifications, and projects increases visibility to potential clients. Creating a personal website or portfolio showcasing completed work, skills, and testimonials from satisfied users demonstrates credibility. A GitHub repository with coding projects, a blog about IT solutions, or a collection of troubleshooting case studies adds value to a freelancer's profile. Clients want to see examples of past work, even if they are personal or volunteer projects, to assess technical abilities and problem-solving skills.

Freelance job platforms are one of the best ways to secure IT gigs. Websites like Upwork, Fiverr, Freelancer, and PeoplePerHour connect freelancers with clients looking for IT services. Creating a profile on these platforms involves writing a compelling description, listing skills, and uploading samples of previous work. New freelancers should start with competitive pricing to attract initial clients and build a reputation through positive reviews. Many successful freelancers began by taking smaller, low-paying projects to gain credibility before increasing their rates. Consistently delivering high-quality work leads to repeat clients and word-of-mouth referrals.

Networking plays a significant role in finding freelance opportunities. Connecting with local businesses, attending IT meetups, and participating in online tech communities can lead to potential clients. Many small businesses need IT assistance but do not have dedicated IT staff. Offering to help with basic tech support, website maintenance, or cloud migration can open doors to freelance contracts. Engaging in discussions on LinkedIn, Reddit, or IT-focused forums helps establish credibility and increases chances of getting recommendations. Building relationships with other freelancers can also lead to subcontracting opportunities on larger projects.

Cold outreach is another effective method for landing freelance gigs. Sending personalized emails or LinkedIn messages to potential clients introducing services and explaining how they can solve technical problems can generate leads. Researching small businesses, startups, or entrepreneurs who may need IT support and offering a free initial consultation or a discounted first project can build trust. Crafting well-written proposals that demonstrate understanding of the client's needs and outline a clear solution improves chances of getting hired. Offering a money-back guarantee or delivering a portion of the work upfront can reassure clients and increase confidence in hiring a new freelancer.

Participating in open-source projects or volunteering IT services for nonprofit organizations can serve as an entry point into freelancing. Contributing to open-source software on GitHub, fixing bugs, or writing documentation provides real-world experience that can be showcased in a portfolio. Nonprofits, community groups, and small businesses often need IT assistance but have limited budgets, making them more open to working with freelancers who are gaining experience. Providing services for free or at a discounted rate initially helps build references, case studies, and practical knowledge that attract paying clients in the future.

Freelancers should continuously improve their skills to remain competitive in the market. Staying updated with the latest technologies, completing relevant certifications, and expanding service offerings help attract more clients. Learning about cybersecurity best practices, automation tools, and cloud platforms can open up higher-paying freelance opportunities. Watching online tutorials, enrolling in IT courses, and practicing in home labs enhance technical abilities and provide additional services that clients may need. Diversifying skills ensures long-term growth and adaptability in the freelance IT industry.

Pricing services appropriately is essential for freelancing success. Beginners may need to start with lower rates to gain experience but should gradually increase pricing as they gain more clients and positive reviews. Researching industry rates, understanding the value of services, and considering the complexity of tasks help determine fair pricing. Offering different pricing structures, such as hourly rates, fixed-price projects, or monthly retainers, gives clients flexibility and increases earning potential. Clear communication about pricing, project scope, and deliverables prevents misunderstandings and ensures smooth client relationships.

Freelancers must also focus on delivering excellent customer service. Timely responses to client inquiries, clear communication about project progress, and meeting deadlines build trust and increase the likelihood of repeat business. Providing detailed documentation, offering after-service support, and ensuring a smooth handover of projects create a positive client experience. Many successful freelancers grow their businesses through client referrals and recommendations, making professionalism and reliability essential qualities.

Managing freelance work effectively involves organization and time management. Using project management tools like Trello, Asana, or Notion helps track deadlines and client requests. Keeping detailed records of tasks, agreements, and payments ensures transparency and prevents disputes. Freelancers should also set boundaries for availability to avoid burnout and maintain work-life balance. Learning how to handle multiple projects efficiently while maintaining quality ensures long-term success in the freelance IT market.

Freelancing in IT offers flexibility, independence, and the opportunity to work on diverse projects. While landing the first gig requires effort, persistence, and strategic positioning, each completed project builds credibility and opens doors to new opportunities. By leveraging online platforms, networking with potential clients, improving skills, and delivering high-quality service, freelancers can establish a successful IT career and transition to more advanced roles or full-time freelancing. The key is to take the first step, gain hands-on experience, and consistently provide value to clients.

Exploring Remote IT Work Opportunities

The rise of remote work has transformed the IT industry, offering professionals the flexibility to work from anywhere while still contributing to technology-driven businesses. Advances in cloud computing, high-speed internet, and collaboration tools have made it possible for IT professionals to perform their tasks without being physically present in an office. Many companies now prefer remote work models, allowing them to access a global talent pool while reducing operational costs. For individuals entering the IT field, remote work opportunities provide a viable path to building a career, gaining experience, and achieving a work-life balance.

One of the biggest advantages of remote IT work is the variety of roles available. Many IT positions, such as software development, cybersecurity analysis, cloud engineering, and technical support, can be performed remotely with minimal disruption. Software developers, for example, can write code, collaborate with teams, and deploy applications from anywhere with an internet connection. Cybersecurity professionals can monitor network activity, conduct penetration testing, and implement security policies without needing to be in an office. Cloud engineers and system administrators can manage virtual machines, configure cloud environments, and troubleshoot infrastructure issues remotely. The flexibility of IT roles makes remote work a natural fit for the industry.

Companies offering remote IT positions often use a combination of tools to ensure smooth communication and collaboration. Video conferencing platforms such as Zoom, Microsoft Teams, and Google Meet facilitate virtual meetings, while messaging apps like Slack and Discord enable instant communication. Project management tools such as Trello, Jira, and Asana help teams stay organized and track progress on assignments. Cloud-based storage services like Google Drive, OneDrive, and Dropbox ensure that important documents and files are accessible from anywhere. Remote IT professionals must become proficient in using these collaboration tools to stay connected with teams and complete their work efficiently.

Finding remote IT job opportunities requires a strategic approach, as competition for these roles is high. Many companies post remote IT job openings on specialized job boards such as We Work Remotely, Remote OK, and FlexJobs. General job sites like LinkedIn, Indeed, and Glassdoor also feature remote IT positions, often listing them with filters that allow job seekers to search for work-from-home opportunities. Creating job alerts and applying to positions early increases the chances of securing interviews, as remote jobs tend to attract a large number of applicants.

Networking plays a significant role in landing remote IT jobs. Engaging with IT professionals, recruiters, and hiring managers on LinkedIn can lead to job referrals and remote work opportunities. Joining remote work communities, participating in online forums, and attending virtual IT conferences provide additional networking avenues. Many companies prefer hiring remote employees through recommendations rather than traditional job applications, making personal connections an essential part of the job search. Reaching out to professionals who already work remotely and seeking advice can provide valuable insights into finding and securing remote IT roles.

Freelancing and contract work are popular ways to gain remote IT experience before securing a full-time remote job. Platforms like Upwork, Freelancer, and Toptal allow IT professionals to find short-term projects that can be completed remotely. Many businesses hire freelancers to handle tasks such as website development, cloud migration, cybersecurity audits, and technical support. Completing freelance projects helps build a portfolio, gain client testimonials, and develop remote work experience that can be highlighted in job applications. Freelancing also provides flexibility, allowing individuals to choose projects that align with their skills and career goals.

For those seeking long-term remote IT employment, it is important to tailor resumes and cover letters to highlight remote work skills. Employers hiring remote workers look for candidates who are self-motivated, disciplined, and capable of working independently. Demonstrating experience with remote collaboration tools, time management, and problem-solving in a remote setting makes a candidate more attractive. Including relevant freelance work, remote internships, or contributions to open-source projects helps showcase the ability to work effectively without direct supervision. Providing clear examples of how technical skills have been applied in a remote setting strengthens a resume and increases the likelihood of getting hired.

Cybersecurity is a major concern for remote IT workers, as working outside a traditional office environment introduces new risks. Companies implement security policies to ensure that remote employees follow best practices for data protection. Using VPNs (Virtual Private Networks) to encrypt connections, enabling multi-factor authentication (MFA) for accounts, and regularly updating software and security patches are essential steps in maintaining cybersecurity. Remote IT professionals must follow company security protocols and take responsibility for protecting sensitive data. Some employers provide secure workstations or require the use of company-managed virtual desktops to minimize security risks.

Time management is a critical skill for remote IT professionals. Without direct supervision, it is essential to stay organized and meet deadlines consistently. Creating a structured daily routine, setting specific work hours, and using productivity tools help maintain focus and efficiency. Techniques such as the Pomodoro method, time-blocking, and setting task priorities ensure that work is completed without unnecessary distractions. Many remote workers use task management apps to break down projects into smaller, manageable steps and track progress. Developing strong time management skills increases productivity and demonstrates reliability to employers.

One of the challenges of remote IT work is maintaining a healthy work-life balance. Without the separation of a physical office, it can be difficult to establish boundaries between work and personal life. Setting up a dedicated workspace, taking regular breaks, and setting clear limits on work hours help create a balanced routine. Engaging in hobbies, exercise, and social activities outside of work prevents burnout and ensures long-term job satisfaction. Remote workers who maintain a structured approach to their workday are more likely to perform effectively and sustain long-term success in remote roles.

Some IT professionals choose to work remotely as digital nomads, traveling while maintaining their jobs. Countries such as Estonia, Portugal, and Thailand offer digital nomad visas, allowing remote workers to live abroad while working for international companies. The ability to work from anywhere appeals to those seeking flexibility and adventure while maintaining a steady income. However, digital nomads must consider factors such as internet reliability, time zone differences, and legal requirements before committing to a remote lifestyle. Researching visa regulations, setting up reliable internet access, and planning work schedules around travel plans are essential for maintaining productivity while working remotely.

Many IT companies are embracing hybrid work models, allowing employees to split their time between remote and in-office work. Hybrid work arrangements provide the benefits of remote flexibility while maintaining access to on-site collaboration when needed. Employees in hybrid roles may work remotely most of the time but visit the office for meetings, training sessions, or major projects. This model allows companies to maintain team cohesion while offering employees the freedom to work from home. Hybrid work is becoming increasingly common in IT, providing an alternative for professionals who enjoy both remote and in-office environments.

The shift toward remote IT work has created opportunities for professionals at all skill levels. Entry-level workers can gain experience through remote internships, freelancing, or contract work, while experienced professionals can secure high-paying remote positions in specialized IT fields. By developing remote work skills, staying organized, networking with industry professionals, and maintaining cybersecurity best practices, IT professionals can successfully navigate the world of remote work. The ability to work remotely provides flexibility, career growth, and access to global job opportunities, making it an attractive option for those looking to build a career in IT.

How to Stay Motivated While Learning IT

Learning IT can be an exciting but challenging journey, especially for beginners who are starting from zero. The field of technology is vast, with countless topics to explore, including programming, networking, cybersecurity, cloud computing, and system administration. While the opportunities in IT are abundant, the learning curve can sometimes feel overwhelming. Many aspiring IT professionals struggle with staying motivated, especially when facing complex concepts, long study hours, and the occasional feeling of stagnation. Developing a strategy to maintain motivation throughout the learning process is essential for long-term success.

Setting clear and realistic goals is one of the most effective ways to stay motivated. Many beginners dive into IT without a structured plan, which can lead to frustration and burnout. Breaking down the learning process into small, achievable milestones helps create a sense of progress. Instead of trying to master an entire programming language or become an expert in networking overnight, focusing on incremental goals, such as completing a specific course, earning a certification, or building a simple project, provides a sense of accomplishment. Writing down goals and tracking progress reinforces motivation and keeps learners engaged in their journey.

Finding a personal reason for learning IT also plays a significant role in maintaining motivation. Some individuals pursue IT for career advancement, higher salaries, or job security, while others have a passion for problem-solving, technology, or innovation. Understanding the deeper motivation behind learning IT helps learners push through difficult moments. Whenever motivation starts to fade, reminding oneself of the long-term benefits, such as better job opportunities, financial stability, and the ability to work in a field with continuous growth, can reignite enthusiasm and commitment to learning.

Developing a structured learning schedule helps maintain consistency and prevents procrastination. Many IT learners, especially self-studiers, struggle with staying on track because they lack a formal schedule. Setting aside dedicated time for studying, practicing, and working on projects ensures steady progress. Whether it is one hour a day or a few hours a week, consistency is more important than intensity. Learning in short, focused sessions rather than cramming long hours reduces fatigue and helps retain information more effectively. A structured routine eliminates the temptation to postpone learning and creates a habit of continuous improvement.

Engaging with the IT community provides valuable support and inspiration. Learning IT can sometimes feel like a solitary journey, but connecting with like-minded individuals makes the experience more enjoyable and motivating. Joining online forums, Discord groups, LinkedIn communities, or local IT meetups allows learners to share progress, ask questions, and get advice from experienced professionals. Being part of a supportive network reduces frustration when facing obstacles and provides encouragement during difficult times. Many learners find that discussing challenges with others who have faced similar struggles helps them stay motivated and gain new insights.

Building real-world projects is a powerful way to stay engaged while learning IT. Many beginners lose motivation because they spend too much time on theoretical concepts without applying their knowledge. Creating personal projects, such as developing a website, setting up a home lab, automating tasks with Python, or configuring a network, helps reinforce learning and makes concepts more tangible. The sense of accomplishment that comes from seeing a project work successfully boosts confidence and keeps learners excited about progressing further. Even small projects that solve everyday problems can provide a strong sense of achievement and encourage continuous learning.

Celebrating small wins is an important aspect of maintaining motivation. The IT learning journey is long, and focusing only on major achievements, such as landing a job, can make the process feel discouraging. Recognizing and rewarding progress, such as mastering a new concept, solving a difficult coding problem, or passing a certification exam, helps maintain enthusiasm. Taking time to appreciate small victories reinforces the idea that every step forward, no matter how small, contributes to overall success. Even something as simple as completing a challenging exercise or debugging an error can be seen as a milestone worth celebrating.

Overcoming the fear of failure is crucial for staying motivated in IT. Many beginners feel discouraged when they struggle to understand a topic, encounter errors in coding, or fail a certification exam. Failure is a natural part of learning, especially in a technical field like IT, where problem-solving is an essential skill. Instead of viewing mistakes as setbacks, learners should see them as opportunities to improve and deepen their understanding. The most successful IT professionals have faced numerous challenges along the way but remained persistent in their learning journey. Adopting a growth mindset, where challenges are seen as learning experiences rather than obstacles, helps maintain long-term motivation.

Taking breaks and avoiding burnout is essential for sustaining motivation over time. Many learners become so focused on studying that they neglect rest, leading to mental fatigue and frustration. Stepping away from screens, engaging in physical activities, and pursuing hobbies outside of IT helps refresh the mind. Short breaks during study sessions improve concentration, while occasional days off prevent burnout. Maintaining a balance between learning and personal life ensures that motivation remains high rather than turning into exhaustion. IT is a field that requires continuous learning, so maintaining long-term energy and enthusiasm is key to success.

Experimenting with different learning resources helps keep the experience fresh and engaging. Some learners may find video tutorials more effective, while others prefer reading books, participating in hands-on labs, or taking interactive courses. If a particular resource feels uninteresting or difficult to follow, switching to another format can reignite enthusiasm. Platforms such as Udemy, Coursera, freeCodeCamp, and YouTube offer diverse learning methods, making it easy to find an approach that suits individual preferences. Exploring different learning styles prevents boredom and helps learners stay engaged throughout their IT journey.

Seeking mentorship from experienced IT professionals provides guidance and motivation. Having a mentor who has already navigated the learning process can offer valuable advice, career insights, and encouragement. Many professionals are willing to share their experiences and support newcomers in the industry. Connecting with mentors through LinkedIn, online communities, or local IT groups can provide direction, prevent common mistakes, and boost confidence. Learning from someone who has successfully built a career in IT helps beginners stay motivated by seeing a clear path to their own success.

Keeping a long-term perspective is important for sustaining motivation in IT. The field is constantly evolving, and learning never truly stops. Instead of focusing solely on reaching a final goal, such as getting a job or becoming an expert, embracing the journey as an ongoing process makes learning more enjoyable. Technology will continue to change, bringing new challenges and opportunities. Viewing IT learning as a continuous adventure rather than a one-time effort helps maintain motivation and excitement for the field.

Learning IT requires dedication, patience, and persistence, but with the right strategies, staying motivated becomes much easier. By setting clear goals, building projects, engaging with the community, and maintaining a balanced approach, learners can keep their enthusiasm alive and enjoy the process of acquiring new skills. The key is to remain consistent, stay curious, and celebrate progress along the way.

Joining Online IT Communities and Forums

Becoming part of an online IT community is one of the most effective ways to accelerate learning, gain industry insights, and connect with experienced professionals. The field of IT is constantly evolving, and keeping up with the latest trends, best practices, and emerging technologies requires continuous engagement. Online forums and communities provide a space for learners, professionals, and experts to share knowledge, ask questions, and collaborate on technical challenges. Whether someone is new to IT or an experienced specialist looking to expand their network, joining these communities can provide valuable support and learning opportunities.

One of the biggest advantages of participating in IT communities is access to real-world problem-solving. Many beginners struggle with technical challenges that may not be covered in formal courses or tutorials. Posting questions on forums allows them to receive guidance from individuals who have encountered similar issues. Platforms such as Stack Overflow, Reddit, and specialized IT forums serve as knowledge bases where technical problems are discussed and resolved. Engaging in these discussions helps learners develop troubleshooting skills, gain exposure to different perspectives, and improve their ability to think critically about technical issues.

Online IT communities also serve as excellent networking tools. Connecting with professionals who work in different areas of IT can open doors to mentorship, job referrals, and career opportunities.

Many IT experts and recruiters participate in these communities, sharing industry insights and offering advice to newcomers. Engaging in discussions, contributing valuable content, and helping others solve problems can help individuals establish a strong online presence. Employers often look for candidates who actively participate in tech communities, as it demonstrates passion, curiosity, and a commitment to continuous learning.

Many IT professionals use forums to stay updated on the latest trends, tools, and industry developments. Technology is constantly evolving, and new software updates, security vulnerabilities, and best practices emerge frequently. Following discussions on platforms such as Hacker News, Tech Twitter, and LinkedIn groups provides instant access to current events in the IT world. Being aware of these developments helps IT professionals stay competitive and adapt to changes in their field. Engaging in conversations about new programming languages, cloud computing advancements, or cybersecurity threats keeps individuals informed and ready for industry shifts.

Participating in coding and technical challenges within IT communities is another great way to enhance skills. Many online groups host competitions, hackathons, and coding challenges where participants can test their problem-solving abilities. Websites such as LeetCode, Codewars, and HackerRank offer coding exercises where developers can practice algorithms, data structures, and system design. Cybersecurity communities like TryHackMe and Hack The Box provide ethical hacking challenges for those interested in penetration testing. Engaging in these activities allows individuals to apply their knowledge in practical scenarios, refine their skills, and gain confidence in their abilities.

For those interested in open-source contributions, IT communities provide opportunities to collaborate on real-world projects. Many software development, cloud computing, and cybersecurity communities maintain open-source repositories that welcome contributions from newcomers. Platforms like GitHub, GitLab, and Bitbucket host collaborative projects where individuals can work on code, improve documentation, and contribute to larger software solutions. Contributing to open-source projects enhances technical skills, builds a portfolio, and demonstrates teamwork and collaboration experience. Many employers value candidates who have contributed to open-source projects, as it shows initiative and practical experience beyond traditional education.

Aside from technical discussions, IT communities provide a space for career guidance and professional development. Many forums have dedicated sections where users can seek advice on job searching, interview preparation, and career transitions. Discussions about certifications, resume building, and salary negotiations help individuals navigate the complexities of the IT job market. Experienced professionals often share their career journeys, providing inspiration and valuable insights for those just starting out. Engaging in these discussions allows individuals to learn from the experiences of others and make informed decisions about their career paths.

Different online platforms cater to various IT specializations, making it important to choose the right community based on personal interests and goals. Stack Overflow is one of the most well-known platforms for developers, offering a vast repository of programming-related questions and answers. Reddit has multiple IT-related subreddits, such as r/learnprogramming for coding beginners, r/sysadmin for system administrators, and r/netsec for cybersecurity professionals. LinkedIn groups provide networking opportunities for professionals looking to connect with industry leaders and recruiters. Discord and Slack communities offer real-time discussions and collaboration spaces for IT enthusiasts.

Engaging in online IT communities requires a proactive approach. Simply joining a forum is not enough; actively participating in discussions, asking thoughtful questions, and offering help to others maximizes the benefits of these platforms. Providing well-researched answers and contributing useful resources builds credibility and establishes a positive reputation within the community. Consistently sharing insights, technical articles, or personal experiences helps individuals become recognized contributors and gain the respect of their peers.

For individuals who may feel intimidated about participating in large IT communities, starting with smaller, niche groups can be a more comfortable approach. Many specialized communities focus on specific technologies, frameworks, or career paths, offering a more focused environment for learning and networking. For example, cloud computing enthusiasts can join AWS or Google Cloud communities, while those interested in ethical hacking can engage with cybersecurity forums and Discord servers. Smaller communities often foster a more supportive and engaging atmosphere, making it easier to build relationships and seek guidance.

Online IT communities also serve as excellent learning resources. Many forums provide tutorials, study guides, and hands-on labs created by experienced professionals. Users often share free learning materials, recommended books, and online courses that help newcomers build foundational knowledge. Engaging in community-led study groups and mentorship programs accelerates learning and provides structured guidance. Many individuals find that learning alongside others in a supportive environment increases motivation and helps them stay accountable for their progress.

Contributing to IT communities not only benefits individuals but also strengthens the collective knowledge base of the industry. Many successful IT professionals started their careers by actively engaging in online forums, sharing knowledge, and collaborating with others. The spirit of knowledge-sharing and collaboration drives innovation and helps newcomers transition into IT roles more smoothly. By giving back to the community through mentorship, answering questions, or writing technical articles, individuals contribute to the growth of the industry while solidifying their own expertise.

Joining online IT communities and forums is one of the most valuable steps for anyone pursuing a career in technology. Whether seeking technical support, career guidance, networking opportunities, or hands-on experience, these communities provide the resources and connections necessary for success. Actively participating, engaging with professionals, and contributing to discussions helps individuals accelerate their learning, build their reputation, and stay informed about industry trends. In a field that thrives on collaboration and innovation, becoming part of a strong IT community is an essential investment in long-term growth and success.

The Importance of Continuous Learning in IT

The IT industry is one of the fastest-evolving fields, requiring professionals to stay updated with new technologies, frameworks, security threats, and best practices. Unlike many other professions where core knowledge remains stable for long periods, IT demands continuous learning to remain relevant. New programming languages, advancements in artificial intelligence, updates in cloud computing, and emerging cybersecurity threats make it essential for IT professionals to develop a habit of lifelong learning. Those who embrace continuous education gain a competitive edge, open doors to better job opportunities, and remain valuable assets to employers.

Technology is constantly changing, and companies rely on IT professionals who can adapt to these changes. Businesses invest in cloud computing, artificial intelligence, cybersecurity, and automation to improve efficiency and security. Professionals who keep up with these innovations position themselves as valuable contributors to their organizations. Employers favor candidates who demonstrate a willingness to learn, as it shows adaptability and a commitment to professional growth. Keeping up with new technologies ensures that IT professionals do not become outdated in a competitive job market where hiring managers seek individuals with the latest skills.

One of the key reasons continuous learning is essential in IT is the rapid evolution of programming languages and software development frameworks. New programming languages emerge, and existing ones receive updates that introduce new features and improvements. Developers who rely solely on one programming language without expanding their knowledge risk limiting their job opportunities. Learning new frameworks and staying updated with industry trends allows developers to work on modern projects and adapt to different environments. Many companies seek full-stack developers who are proficient in multiple languages and frameworks, making continuous learning a critical part of career advancement.

Cybersecurity is another area where continuous learning is necessary. Cyber threats evolve daily, and attackers constantly find new vulnerabilities to exploit. IT professionals responsible for securing systems, networks, and applications must stay ahead of these threats by learning about the latest attack techniques and defense strategies. Security certifications, ethical hacking courses, and hands-on practice with penetration testing tools help cybersecurity professionals remain effective in protecting digital assets. Organizations rely on security experts who can implement up-to-date security measures, monitor for vulnerabilities, and respond to emerging threats. Without continuous learning, cybersecurity professionals may fail to recognize new risks and leave systems vulnerable to attacks.

Cloud computing has transformed the way businesses manage IT infrastructure, requiring IT professionals to learn new cloud technologies and services. Companies increasingly migrate to cloud platforms such as Amazon Web Services (AWS), Microsoft Azure, and Google Cloud to improve scalability and reduce costs. IT professionals must stay informed about cloud computing best practices, security measures, and automation tools to manage cloud environments effectively. Obtaining cloud certifications and gaining hands-on experience with cloud platforms enhances career prospects and allows IT professionals to take advantage of remote and global job opportunities.

Automation and artificial intelligence are reshaping various IT roles, making continuous learning a necessity for staying relevant. Many traditional IT tasks, such as system administration, network configuration, and software testing, are becoming automated. IT professionals who understand automation tools, scripting languages, and AI-driven solutions can streamline workflows and improve efficiency. Learning how to use tools such as Ansible, Terraform, and machine learning frameworks allows professionals to automate repetitive tasks, freeing up time for more complex problem-solving. Embracing automation skills ensures that IT professionals remain valuable as technology continues to evolve.

Continuous learning in IT is not limited to technical skills; it also involves improving problem-solving, communication, and project management abilities. Many IT roles require professionals to collaborate with teams, explain technical concepts to non-technical stakeholders, and manage projects efficiently. Learning soft skills such as leadership, teamwork, and adaptability enhances an IT professional's effectiveness in the workplace. Strong communication skills help developers, network engineers, and security analysts convey their ideas clearly, making collaboration easier. Investing in personal development alongside technical education creates well-rounded IT professionals who can contribute beyond their technical expertise.

Certifications play a significant role in continuous learning and career advancement in IT. Many employers require certifications as proof of knowledge and expertise in specific areas. Earning certifications such as CompTIA A+, Network+, Security+, Cisco's CCNA, AWS Certified Solutions Architect, and Certified Ethical Hacker (CEH) demonstrates competency in relevant IT domains. Certifications validate skills, increase credibility, and improve job prospects. Since certification requirements evolve over time, IT professionals must stay informed about new exam objectives and industry standards. Maintaining certifications and earning new ones keeps skills sharp and ensures continued professional growth.

Engaging in IT communities and attending industry events enhances continuous learning by providing exposure to new ideas, technologies, and best practices. Many IT professionals participate in conferences, webinars, and online communities to stay connected with industry trends. Attending events such as DEF CON, AWS re:Invent, and Google Cloud Next allows IT professionals to learn from experts, network with peers, and gain hands-on experience with cutting-edge technology. Online forums, LinkedIn groups, and Discord communities provide ongoing discussions about industry developments, helping professionals stay updated on relevant topics.

Experimenting with personal projects is one of the best ways to reinforce continuous learning. Many IT professionals build their own software applications, set up home labs, or contribute to open-source projects to practice new skills. Working on side projects allows individuals to explore emerging technologies without the constraints of a work environment. Developers may create web applications using new frameworks, network engineers may configure virtual lab environments, and cybersecurity professionals may test penetration testing tools on simulated networks. Practical experience gained from hands-on projects deepens understanding and strengthens problem-solving abilities.

Online learning platforms provide convenient access to continuous education, allowing IT professionals to learn new skills at their own pace. Websites such as Udemy, Coursera, Pluralsight, and freeCodeCamp offer courses on programming, cybersecurity, cloud computing, and system administration. Many courses include hands-on labs, quizzes, and real-world projects that reinforce learning. Staying committed to self-improvement through online courses ensures that IT professionals remain competitive and adaptable in their careers.

Mentorship is another valuable aspect of continuous learning in IT. Seeking guidance from experienced professionals provides insights into career paths, best practices, and industry expectations. Mentors can recommend resources, provide feedback on technical projects, and offer advice on career progression. Many IT professionals find mentors through networking events, online communities, and workplace relationships. Learning from someone with experience accelerates growth, reduces the likelihood of common mistakes, and provides motivation to keep progressing.

Continuous learning is essential for long-term success in IT. Those who remain proactive in acquiring new skills, adapting to industry changes, and expanding their knowledge will have greater career opportunities. The most successful IT professionals embrace learning as an ongoing process, recognizing that technology will always evolve. Developing a habit of continuous education ensures that IT professionals stay relevant, competitive, and prepared for future advancements in the industry.

Avoiding Common Beginner Mistakes in IT Careers

Starting a career in IT can be exciting, but many beginners make common mistakes that can slow down their progress and create unnecessary frustration. IT is a vast and constantly evolving field, and navigating it without proper guidance can lead to missteps that hinder professional growth. Understanding these mistakes and how to avoid them can help aspiring IT professionals build a strong foundation, stay motivated, and achieve long-term success. Recognizing potential pitfalls early in the journey ensures that beginners make informed decisions, develop good habits, and maximize their learning opportunities.

One of the biggest mistakes beginners make is trying to learn too many things at once. IT offers numerous career paths, including programming, networking, cybersecurity, cloud computing, and system administration. Many newcomers get overwhelmed by the vast number of technologies and attempt to learn multiple subjects simultaneously. This often leads to frustration and a lack of deep understanding in any one area. A better approach is to focus on a specific field, master its fundamentals, and gradually expand knowledge over time. Starting with a structured learning path, such as mastering networking basics before diving into cybersecurity, helps build a solid foundation.

Another common mistake is neglecting hands-on practice. Many beginners focus too much on theoretical knowledge without applying what they learn in real-world scenarios. Reading books, watching tutorials, and taking online courses are important, but practical experience is what solidifies skills. IT professionals are expected to troubleshoot problems, configure systems, and write efficient code. Setting up home labs, experimenting with virtual machines, contributing to open-source projects, and working on small coding exercises are essential for reinforcing learning. Employers value candidates who can demonstrate practical experience rather than just theoretical understanding.

Many beginners also fall into the trap of relying solely on certifications without developing practical skills. Certifications are valuable in IT, as they validate knowledge and improve job prospects. However, some individuals focus only on passing certification exams without fully understanding the concepts behind them. Memorizing answers for tests does not translate into real-world competence. It is crucial to supplement certification studies with hands-on projects, lab exercises, and real-world problem-solving. Hiring managers prefer candidates who can apply their knowledge in practical situations rather than just listing certifications on a resume.

Ignoring soft skills is another mistake that can limit career growth in IT. While technical expertise is essential, communication, teamwork, problem-solving, and adaptability are equally important. Many IT roles involve working with teams, interacting with clients, and explaining technical concepts to non-technical stakeholders. Beginners who focus solely on technical knowledge without improving their interpersonal skills may struggle in workplace environments. Practicing clear communication, participating in team projects, and developing customer service skills help IT professionals succeed in collaborative work settings. Soft skills often make the difference between a good technician and a great IT professional.

Failing to document work and take notes is another common mistake. Many beginners rely on memory instead of keeping a record of troubleshooting steps, commands, and solutions. In IT, documenting processes and solutions helps streamline future work and prevents repetitive mistakes. Keeping a personal knowledge base, using note-taking apps, or maintaining a blog with technical write-ups improves efficiency and reinforces learning. Professionals who document their work develop strong troubleshooting skills and build a valuable resource for themselves and others. Good documentation habits also help in career growth, as they demonstrate organization and attention to detail.

Neglecting networking and professional connections is another misstep that beginners often make. Many IT professionals land their first job or internship through networking rather than traditional applications. Attending industry events, joining online communities, participating in LinkedIn discussions, and engaging in mentorship programs can open doors to job opportunities. Beginners who isolate themselves miss out on valuable career advice, job referrals, and industry insights. Building professional relationships and seeking guidance from experienced IT professionals accelerates career growth and provides long-term benefits.

Many beginners underestimate the importance of cybersecurity best practices. IT professionals are responsible for protecting systems, networks, and sensitive data. Ignoring security fundamentals, such as using weak passwords, failing to update software, or not enabling two-factor authentication, can lead to serious security breaches. Practicing good cybersecurity hygiene from the beginning helps build responsible habits. Understanding common threats, learning encryption techniques, and following security best practices ensures that IT professionals contribute to safe and secure digital environments. Employers expect IT professionals to prioritize security in their work.

Another frequent mistake is expecting immediate results and giving up too soon. Learning IT skills takes time, and progress is not always linear. Many beginners become discouraged when they struggle with complex topics, encounter errors, or feel stuck. It is important to embrace challenges as part of the learning process. Every experienced IT professional has faced difficulties, but persistence and problem-solving lead to improvement. Breaking down difficult concepts, seeking help from online communities, and revisiting foundational topics help overcome obstacles. Developing resilience and patience is crucial for long-term success in IT.

Some beginners also overlook the importance of version control and backup strategies. Developers should learn Git early in their journey to manage code changes and collaborate effectively. System administrators and network engineers should implement proper backup solutions to prevent data loss. Many IT professionals have faced situations where hours of work were lost due to a lack of version control or backup policies. Learning how to use Git repositories, setting up automated backups, and understanding disaster recovery principles are essential skills that prevent unnecessary setbacks.

Failing to adapt to industry changes is another mistake that can limit career advancement. IT evolves rapidly, and technologies that are popular today may become obsolete in a few years. Beginners who focus on outdated skills or refuse to learn new tools risk falling behind. Staying updated with industry trends, exploring emerging technologies, and continuously learning new skills ensures long-term career growth. Following IT news, participating in training programs, and experimenting with new technologies help IT professionals remain competitive.

Overcomplicating solutions is another pitfall for beginners. Many new IT professionals try to implement complex fixes when simpler solutions exist. Understanding the core principles of problem-solving and troubleshooting is more important than using advanced techniques unnecessarily. IT professionals should follow the principle of keeping solutions simple and effective. Overcomplicating scripts, configurations, or code can introduce unnecessary issues and make maintenance more difficult. Learning to analyze problems carefully and apply straightforward solutions improves efficiency and reliability.

A final mistake that many beginners make is undervaluing job experience, even in non-technical roles. Many individuals wait for the perfect IT job instead of gaining experience in related positions. Customer support roles, technical internships, and freelance projects all provide valuable experience that can lead to better opportunities. Employers value candidates who have worked in technical environments, even if their initial roles were not their ideal jobs. Gaining any form of IT-related experience helps build confidence, improves technical abilities, and increases job prospects.

Avoiding these common beginner mistakes helps aspiring IT professionals navigate their careers more effectively. By focusing on practical skills, networking, documentation, cybersecurity, and continuous learning, beginners can build a strong foundation for long-term success. Learning IT is a journey, and avoiding these pitfalls ensures a smoother path toward professional growth, confidence, and expertise in the field.

Learning from IT Failure and Troubleshooting

Failure is an inevitable part of working in IT. No matter how skilled a professional becomes, mistakes will happen, systems will break, and unexpected issues will arise. What separates a great IT professional from an average one is the ability to learn from these failures and develop effective troubleshooting skills. IT careers revolve around solving technical problems, fixing broken systems, and preventing future issues. Embracing failure as a learning opportunity rather than a setback helps IT professionals build resilience, sharpen their problem-solving abilities, and improve their overall expertise.

Troubleshooting is one of the most critical skills in IT, as almost every role requires diagnosing and resolving issues. System administrators deal with server failures, network engineers fix connectivity problems, software developers debug code errors, and cybersecurity professionals investigate security breaches. Learning how to approach problems systematically is essential for success in any IT field. Many beginners make the mistake of guessing solutions instead of following a structured troubleshooting process. Developing a methodical approach to problem-solving leads to more efficient and accurate resolutions.

One of the first steps in troubleshooting is identifying the problem accurately. Many IT failures appear to be one issue but are actually caused by something deeper. For example, a network outage might seem like a router failure when the real cause is a misconfigured firewall rule. A slow computer might be diagnosed as a hardware problem when it is actually due to background applications consuming excessive resources. Understanding the exact symptoms of a failure and gathering as much information as possible before attempting a fix prevents unnecessary changes that could make the problem worse.

Asking the right questions is a key part of troubleshooting. What was the system's last known working state? Did anything change before the failure occurred? Are there any error messages or logs that provide clues? Have similar issues happened before? Gathering this information helps narrow down potential causes and avoids wasted time testing unrelated solutions. IT professionals who develop strong questioning skills become more efficient at diagnosing and resolving issues. Many problems have clear patterns that can be identified by analyzing past experiences and comparing symptoms to known issues.

Using logical deduction and elimination is an effective troubleshooting technique. Instead of randomly changing settings or rebooting systems without understanding the issue, IT professionals should systematically test different components to isolate the root cause. For example, if a network issue affects multiple devices, testing connectivity at different points in the network helps determine whether the problem is with the router, a switch, or an individual device. If a software application crashes frequently, testing different versions, checking compatibility, and analyzing system logs helps pinpoint the cause. Isolating variables through step-by-step testing prevents unnecessary changes that could introduce new problems.

Documenting failures and solutions is an essential practice in IT troubleshooting. Many professionals encounter the same issues multiple times, and keeping a record of past problems saves time in future troubleshooting efforts. Writing down error messages, the steps taken to resolve the issue, and any lessons learned creates a personal knowledge base that can be referenced later. Many IT teams maintain documentation systems where solutions are shared among colleagues, helping everyone learn from each other's experiences. Well-documented troubleshooting steps also make it easier to train new team members and ensure consistency in handling technical issues.

Understanding that failure is an opportunity for growth is crucial for IT professionals. Many individuals, especially beginners, feel discouraged when they encounter complex problems they cannot immediately solve. However, every difficult troubleshooting situation provides a chance to gain new knowledge. Fixing a critical server failure, resolving a difficult programming bug, or recovering from a security incident teaches valuable lessons that cannot be learned from books or courses alone. IT professionals who embrace these challenges become more confident in their abilities and develop the problem-solving mindset necessary for long-term success.

Seeking help and learning from others is an important part of troubleshooting. Many IT professionals make the mistake of struggling with a problem for too long without reaching out for assistance. Online forums, IT communities, and professional networks provide valuable resources for solving complex issues. Platforms like Stack Overflow, Reddit, and vendor support forums allow professionals to find solutions, ask for guidance, and learn from experts who have encountered similar problems. Collaborating with colleagues, discussing challenges in team meetings, and attending technical workshops also provide opportunities to gain insights and improve troubleshooting skills.

Developing a structured approach to troubleshooting minimizes stress and improves efficiency. Many IT professionals follow established frameworks, such as the divide-and-conquer method, where large problems are broken down into smaller, more manageable parts. For example, when diagnosing a software issue, separating problems related to hardware, operating systems, and applications helps pinpoint the cause more quickly. Another common approach is the bottom-up or top-down method in network troubleshooting, where problems are analyzed starting from either the physical layer or the application layer, depending on the situation. Following structured methodologies ensures that problems are solved logically rather than through trial and error.

Testing and verifying fixes before implementing them in production environments is another critical aspect of troubleshooting. Many IT failures are caused by rushed solutions that introduce unintended consequences. Making changes without proper testing can result in data loss, system downtime, or security vulnerabilities. IT professionals should use test environments, virtual machines, and backup systems to validate fixes before applying them to critical systems. Creating rollback plans ensures that if a solution does not work as expected, the system can be restored to its previous state without major disruptions.

Preventing recurring failures is just as important as resolving them. Many IT professionals spend time fixing the same issues repeatedly because underlying problems are not addressed. Instead of applying temporary fixes, identifying and resolving root causes prevents future incidents. For example, if a server crashes due to insufficient resources, upgrading hardware or optimizing software usage provides a long-term solution rather than continuously restarting the server. Proactive maintenance, performance monitoring, and regular system updates reduce the likelihood of failures and improve overall reliability.

Troubleshooting extends beyond technical knowledge; it requires patience, persistence, and a willingness to experiment. Some IT failures are straightforward, while others require extensive research and testing. Professionals who develop a problem-solving mindset approach each challenge as a puzzle rather than a frustration. Breaking down complex issues, testing different hypotheses, and analyzing results with a logical mindset lead to more effective solutions. The ability to remain calm under pressure, think critically, and adapt to unexpected problems is what makes a successful IT professional.

Every failure in IT presents a learning opportunity. Whether it is a software crash, a security breach, or a network outage, each incident provides valuable insights that contribute to professional growth. Troubleshooting is an ongoing process that improves with experience, and IT professionals who develop strong troubleshooting skills become highly valuable in their careers. By embracing challenges, seeking solutions methodically, and continuously improving technical knowledge, IT professionals can turn failures into stepping stones for long-term success.

How to Transition from IT Support to Other Roles

Many IT professionals begin their careers in IT support roles, assisting users with technical issues, troubleshooting hardware and software problems, and maintaining IT systems. While IT support provides a strong foundation in problem-solving, customer service, and technical troubleshooting, many professionals eventually seek to transition into more specialized roles such as network administration, cybersecurity, software development, cloud computing, or data analysis. Making this transition requires a combination of skill development, hands-on experience, certifications, networking, and strategic career planning. Understanding the steps necessary to move beyond IT support helps professionals take control of their career paths and open new opportunities in the IT field.

The first step in transitioning from IT support is identifying a target role based on interests, strengths, and long-term career goals. IT is a broad industry with many different career paths, and choosing the right one depends on personal preferences and skills. Those who enjoy troubleshooting network issues may consider a career in network administration or network engineering. Individuals interested in security threats and data protection might explore cybersecurity roles. Professionals who enjoy coding and automation may transition into software development or DevOps. Choosing a clear path allows for focused learning and skill-building rather than attempting to learn everything at once.

Once a target career path is chosen, acquiring the necessary technical skills is essential. IT support provides exposure to fundamental technical concepts, but specialized roles require deeper expertise. For network administration, learning networking protocols, configuring routers and switches, and understanding firewall management is crucial. Cybersecurity roles require knowledge of penetration testing, threat analysis, and security frameworks. Software development demands proficiency in programming languages, data structures, and software engineering principles. Learning relevant skills through online courses, certifications, books, and hands-on practice bridges the gap between IT support and specialized roles.

Hands-on experience is a critical component of transitioning from IT support. Many specialized roles require practical knowledge that cannot be gained through theory alone. Setting up a home lab, working on personal projects, and contributing to open-source initiatives provide valuable experience. Aspiring network administrators can practice configuring network devices using Cisco Packet Tracer or GNS3. Those interested in cybersecurity can participate in Capture The Flag (CTF) competitions and ethical hacking challenges on platforms like TryHackMe or Hack The Box. Software developers can build applications, contribute to GitHub repositories, and automate tasks with scripting. Demonstrating real-world experience in a portfolio increases credibility when applying for new roles.

Certifications play a significant role in making the transition from IT support to other IT careers. Many specialized roles have industry-recognized certifications that validate skills and knowledge. For network administration, certifications like CompTIA Network+, Cisco CCNA, and Juniper JNCIA help establish networking expertise. Cybersecurity professionals benefit from earning CompTIA Security+, Certified Ethical Hacker (CEH), or CISSP. Cloud computing aspirants can pursue AWS Certified Solutions Architect, Microsoft Azure Fundamentals, or Google Cloud certifications. Software developers may focus on coding certifications or demonstrate their expertise through coding challenges and projects. Earning certifications increases job market competitiveness and helps professionals stand out to potential employers.

On-the-job learning and internal career advancement opportunities can accelerate the transition from IT support. Many organizations encourage employees to grow within the company and offer training programs, mentorship, and role transitions. Expressing interest in other IT roles to managers, volunteering for cross-department projects, and taking on additional responsibilities can lead to internal promotions. Helping with networking configurations, security audits, or scripting automation tasks in the current job role provides hands-on experience while gaining recognition from supervisors. Demonstrating initiative and a willingness to learn makes it easier for IT support professionals to move into higher-level technical positions within the same company.

Networking is a powerful tool for transitioning from IT support to other roles. Building relationships with professionals in the desired career field provides insights, mentorship, and job opportunities. Engaging in LinkedIn discussions, attending IT conferences, and joining professional organizations expand professional networks. Connecting with hiring managers, recruiters, and industry experts increases the chances of finding opportunities in specialized IT fields. Many IT professionals land new roles through referrals rather than traditional job applications, making networking an essential part of career growth. Seeking guidance from mentors who have successfully transitioned from IT support can provide valuable advice and direction.

Gaining coding and automation skills can significantly improve career prospects for IT support professionals transitioning into roles such as system administration, DevOps, and cloud engineering. Learning scripting languages like Python, PowerShell, or Bash helps automate repetitive tasks and enhances efficiency. Understanding infrastructure as code (IaC) tools such as Terraform and Ansible provides valuable skills for cloud and DevOps positions. Many organizations seek professionals who can integrate automation into IT operations, making scripting and coding abilities a valuable asset when transitioning to more technical roles.

Soft skills remain important even when moving into specialized IT roles. IT support professionals develop strong customer service, communication, and problem-solving skills, which are valuable in any IT career. Security analysts need to explain risks to executives, network engineers collaborate with teams to design infrastructure, and software developers must communicate project requirements effectively. Highlighting these skills when applying for new roles shows adaptability and readiness for more advanced positions. Technical expertise combined with strong interpersonal skills creates a well-rounded IT professional capable of excelling in any field.

Applying for specialized roles requires a strategic approach to resume building and job applications. Tailoring resumes to highlight relevant skills, certifications, and hands-on projects demonstrates readiness for the target position. Including keywords from job descriptions increases the chances of passing applicant tracking systems (ATS) used by employers. Showcasing a portfolio with projects, GitHub repositories, and certification badges provides concrete proof of technical abilities. Writing cover letters that explain the transition from IT support and emphasize transferable skills helps create a compelling job application. Persistence in applying for roles and preparing for technical interviews ensures a higher chance of securing a specialized IT job.

Staying updated with industry trends and advancements is crucial during the transition. Technology evolves rapidly, and keeping up with new developments ensures relevance in the job market. Following tech blogs, participating in online courses, and engaging with IT communities provide ongoing learning opportunities. Many IT professionals continue self-improvement even after securing a specialized role to maintain career growth. Remaining curious, adaptable, and proactive about learning ensures long-term success in any IT career path.

The transition from IT support to a specialized IT role requires dedication, continuous learning, and strategic career planning. By acquiring technical skills, gaining hands-on experience, earning certifications, leveraging networking opportunities, and demonstrating initiative, IT support professionals can successfully move into more advanced positions. Building a clear roadmap, staying committed to professional development, and taking proactive steps toward career growth ensures a smooth and rewarding transition into the next phase of an IT career.

Developing Your Problem-Solving Skills in IT

Problem-solving is one of the most important skills in IT, as nearly every role in the field requires identifying, analyzing, and resolving technical issues. Whether working in software development, networking, cybersecurity, or technical support, IT professionals must develop the ability to approach complex problems logically and efficiently. Strong problem-solving skills not only improve performance in day-to-day tasks but also make professionals more valuable to their teams and organizations. Developing a structured approach to troubleshooting, enhancing critical thinking, and practicing real-world scenarios help IT professionals sharpen their problem-solving abilities and excel in their careers.

A structured approach to problem-solving is essential for efficiency and accuracy. Many IT professionals follow established methodologies to break down complex issues into manageable parts. One of the most commonly used techniques is the divide-and-conquer method, where a large problem is broken into smaller sections to isolate the root cause. For example, when troubleshooting a network issue, identifying whether the problem lies in hardware, software, or configuration settings helps narrow the focus and speeds up resolution. This method allows IT professionals to systematically eliminate possible causes rather than relying on guesswork.

Another effective approach is the step-by-step diagnostic method, which involves testing one potential solution at a time and verifying the results before proceeding. This prevents unnecessary changes that could introduce new problems. For instance, if a user reports that their computer is not connecting to the internet, checking physical connections, verifying network settings, testing on another device, and reviewing error messages provide valuable clues. Making one change at a time ensures that IT professionals understand the impact of each adjustment and avoid making the problem worse.

Critical thinking plays a significant role in problem-solving, as it allows IT professionals to analyze situations logically and evaluate multiple solutions. Instead of immediately jumping to conclusions, taking a moment to assess the issue, consider alternative explanations, and predict potential outcomes leads to more effective resolutions. Many IT problems have multiple possible causes, and critical thinking helps determine which solutions are most likely to succeed based on available evidence. Developing the habit of questioning assumptions and verifying information improves decision-making and leads to better troubleshooting outcomes.

Practicing real-world problem-solving scenarios enhances IT professionals' ability to think quickly and adapt to unexpected challenges. Hands-on experience, such as setting up virtual labs, participating in technical challenges, or experimenting with different configurations, provides valuable insights into how systems behave under different conditions. Many cybersecurity professionals, for example, sharpen their skills through Capture The Flag (CTF) competitions, which simulate real-world hacking and security challenges. Similarly, network engineers practice troubleshooting by configuring routers and switches in virtual environments. Engaging in these practical exercises builds confidence and improves problem-solving efficiency in professional settings.

Documentation is another essential aspect of problem-solving in IT. Keeping detailed records of troubleshooting steps, solutions, and outcomes helps IT professionals learn from past experiences and avoid repeating mistakes. Many IT teams maintain knowledge bases, internal wikis, or ticketing systems where solutions to common problems are documented for future reference. Writing down the thought process behind solving a problem reinforces understanding and allows others to benefit from shared knowledge. IT professionals who develop strong documentation habits become more effective at diagnosing and resolving issues over time.

Collaboration and knowledge sharing also contribute to problem-solving development. IT professionals often work in teams, and leveraging collective expertise leads to faster and more efficient resolutions. Seeking input from colleagues, discussing technical challenges in online forums, and participating in IT communities provide access to diverse perspectives and solutions. Many complex IT problems have been solved through open discussions where different professionals contribute insights based on their experiences. Learning from others and being open to feedback enhances problem-solving skills and broadens technical knowledge.

Time management is an important factor in problem-solving, especially when working under pressure. IT professionals often deal with urgent issues that require quick resolutions to minimize downtime and maintain system availability. Developing the ability to prioritize tasks, manage stress, and stay focused ensures that problems are handled efficiently. Understanding when to escalate an issue to a more experienced colleague or seek additional resources prevents wasted time on problems that require specialized expertise. Balancing speed with accuracy ensures that solutions are implemented effectively without compromising system stability.

Automation and scripting help streamline problem-solving by reducing repetitive tasks and increasing efficiency. IT professionals who learn scripting languages like Python, PowerShell, or Bash can automate troubleshooting processes, log analysis, and system monitoring. For example, instead of manually checking server logs for errors, writing a script to automatically scan logs and flag anomalies saves time and reduces human error. Automating routine troubleshooting tasks allows IT professionals to focus on solving more complex problems while improving overall system reliability.

Understanding root cause analysis is essential for preventing recurring problems. Many IT professionals encounter situations where the same issues arise repeatedly because the underlying cause is not addressed. Instead of applying temporary fixes, identifying the root cause ensures that long-term solutions are implemented. For example, if a server crashes frequently, simply restarting it each time does not solve the real issue. Investigating hardware performance, checking resource usage, and reviewing system logs provide deeper insights into why the failure occurs. Addressing the root cause prevents future incidents and improves system stability.

Exposure to different IT environments and technologies broadens problem-solving skills by introducing new challenges and learning opportunities. Working on diverse projects, experimenting with different operating systems, and exploring cloud computing platforms provide valuable experience in handling various technical issues. IT professionals who diversify their knowledge and gain exposure to multiple technologies become more adaptable and capable of solving a wider range of problems. Staying curious and continuously learning ensures that IT professionals remain prepared for new challenges in the ever-evolving technology landscape.

Effective communication is often overlooked in IT problem-solving, but it plays a crucial role in finding and implementing solutions. Many IT professionals need to explain technical issues to non-technical users, collaborate with team members, or document solutions for future reference. Clear and concise communication ensures that problems are accurately reported, solutions are well understood, and troubleshooting steps are effectively shared. IT professionals who develop strong communication skills enhance their ability to work with different teams and improve overall problem-solving efficiency.

Developing problem-solving skills in IT requires practice, persistence, and a willingness to embrace challenges. By following structured troubleshooting approaches, enhancing critical thinking, gaining hands-on experience, collaborating with others, and leveraging automation, IT professionals can improve their ability to diagnose and resolve issues efficiently. The ability to solve complex problems is a defining characteristic of successful IT professionals, making it one of the most valuable skills to cultivate in any technology career.

Understanding IT Project Management Basics

IT project management is an essential discipline that ensures technology initiatives are successfully planned, executed, and delivered on time and within budget. Unlike traditional project management, IT project management involves managing software development, infrastructure upgrades, cybersecurity initiatives, cloud migrations, and other technology-related projects. IT professionals who understand the fundamentals of project management can effectively coordinate teams, allocate resources, mitigate risks, and ensure project success. Learning the basics of IT project management helps professionals improve efficiency, collaborate better with teams, and contribute to organizational success.

Every IT project begins with project initiation, where the project goals, scope, and stakeholders are defined. During this phase, project managers work with stakeholders to determine the problem that needs to be solved, identify key objectives, and establish the project's overall direction. Clearly defining the project's scope ensures that expectations are aligned and prevents scope creep, which occurs when additional requirements are introduced without proper planning. A well-defined project initiation phase lays the foundation for a structured approach to execution and ensures that all team members understand their roles and responsibilities.

The planning phase is one of the most critical stages of IT project management. In this phase, project managers develop a roadmap that outlines the tasks, timelines, resources, and dependencies required to complete the project. Detailed planning includes breaking down the project into manageable tasks, estimating the time and effort needed for each component, and assigning responsibilities to team members. Many IT projects use methodologies such as Agile or Waterfall to structure their approach. Agile focuses on iterative development and continuous feedback, while Waterfall follows a sequential process where each phase is completed before moving on to the next. Choosing the right methodology depends on the nature of the project and the organization's preferences.

Risk management is an important aspect of IT project planning. Identifying potential risks, such as technical challenges, security vulnerabilities, or resource limitations, allows teams to develop contingency plans and minimize disruptions. IT projects often face unexpected challenges, such as software compatibility issues, changing business requirements, or security threats. Having a proactive risk management strategy ensures that the project remains on track even when obstacles arise. Regular risk assessments and contingency planning help teams address potential problems before they escalate into major issues.

The execution phase is where the actual work of the project takes place. During this phase, developers write code, network engineers configure infrastructure, security teams implement security measures, and other IT professionals contribute their expertise to complete assigned tasks. Effective communication is essential during execution to ensure that team members stay aligned and collaborate efficiently. Regular meetings, progress reports, and status updates help keep stakeholders informed about the project's progress. Many IT teams use collaboration tools such as Jira, Trello, or Microsoft Teams to track tasks, assign responsibilities, and ensure that work is progressing according to the plan.

One of the biggest challenges in IT project management is managing changing requirements. Unlike traditional projects, where requirements are often fixed from the beginning, IT projects frequently evolve based on stakeholder feedback, emerging technologies, and shifting business needs. Agile methodologies, such as Scrum, provide a flexible approach that allows teams to adapt to changes while maintaining project momentum. Regular sprint planning meetings, retrospectives, and feedback loops ensure that adjustments can be made without disrupting the overall project timeline. Adapting to change while maintaining project objectives is a key skill in IT project management.

The monitoring and control phase ensures that the project stays on track and meets its intended goals. Project managers continuously monitor progress, track key performance indicators (KPIs), and address any deviations from the original plan. Performance metrics, such as completion percentages, issue resolution rates, and resource utilization, help assess the project's overall health. If problems arise, corrective actions are taken to bring the project back on course. Effective monitoring helps identify inefficiencies, bottlenecks, and risks early in the process, allowing teams to make data-driven decisions and improve project outcomes.

Communication plays a crucial role in IT project management. Clear and effective communication between team members, stakeholders, and management ensures that everyone is aligned and working towards common goals. Miscommunication can lead to misunderstandings, missed deadlines, and conflicts within the team. IT project managers must ensure that all project updates, requirements, and expectations are conveyed clearly and consistently. Regular meetings, written documentation, and collaboration platforms help facilitate effective communication throughout the project lifecycle.

Budgeting and resource management are essential components of IT project success. Many IT projects require investments in software, hardware, cloud services, and personnel. Allocating resources efficiently ensures that the project remains financially viable while delivering expected results. Overspending or underestimating costs can lead to project delays, financial strain, or the inability to complete critical tasks. IT project managers must carefully plan budgets, track expenditures, and make data-driven decisions to optimize resource allocation. Proper financial management ensures that the project stays within budget and meets organizational expectations.

The testing and quality assurance phase ensures that the project meets its intended objectives and functions correctly. In IT projects, testing is crucial for identifying bugs, security vulnerabilities, and performance issues before deployment. Software development projects undergo unit testing, integration testing, and user acceptance testing (UAT) to validate functionality. Infrastructure projects require performance testing, security assessments, and system validations to ensure reliability. Quality assurance teams play a critical role in maintaining project integrity and delivering a final product that meets user expectations.

The final stage of an IT project is the deployment and closure phase. Once all tasks are completed, and testing is successful, the project is deployed for use. Deployment may involve rolling out new software, configuring new systems, or implementing security measures. Post-deployment support is often required to address any issues that arise after implementation. IT project managers conduct post-project evaluations to analyze lessons learned, identify areas for improvement, and document best practices for future projects. Closing a project properly ensures that all stakeholders are satisfied, documentation is completed, and resources are reallocated efficiently.

Continuous improvement is a key principle in IT project management. Every completed project provides valuable insights into what worked well and what could be improved. Conducting post-mortem reviews, gathering feedback from team members, and refining project management processes contribute to long-term success. Organizations that focus on continuous improvement enhance their ability to deliver successful IT projects, reduce inefficiencies, and adapt to changing technological landscapes. IT professionals who embrace learning from past projects improve their management skills and increase their chances of leading future successful initiatives.

Understanding IT project management basics is essential for anyone involved in IT initiatives. Whether working as a developer, network engineer, cybersecurity professional, or IT manager, knowing how to structure, execute, and monitor projects improves efficiency and collaboration. Developing project management skills allows IT professionals to take on leadership roles, contribute to strategic decision-making, and drive technology projects that deliver real business value. By mastering these fundamental principles, IT professionals can ensure that projects are completed successfully while meeting organizational goals and stakeholder expectations.

Learning About DevOps and System Administration

DevOps and system administration are two essential fields in IT that focus on managing infrastructure, automating processes, and ensuring the smooth operation of computer systems. While system administration has traditionally been responsible for maintaining servers, networks, and IT environments, DevOps has emerged as a modern approach that integrates development and operations to improve collaboration, automation, and software deployment efficiency. Understanding these roles and their key principles helps IT professionals build a strong foundation for managing systems, improving reliability, and streamlining IT processes.

System administration involves configuring, maintaining, and troubleshooting computer systems, networks, and servers. System administrators, often referred to as sysadmins, are responsible for ensuring that IT infrastructure runs efficiently, securely, and without interruptions. Their tasks include managing user accounts, setting up operating systems, applying security updates, and monitoring system performance. Sysadmins work with various operating systems, such as Windows Server and Linux, and must have expertise in configuring services like Active Directory, DNS, DHCP, and virtualization platforms. Keeping systems updated, performing backups, and responding to incidents are critical responsibilities of a system administrator.

A system administrator must have strong knowledge of networking concepts since many IT systems rely on secure and stable network connectivity. Understanding IP addressing, routing, firewalls, and network protocols such as TCP/IP, HTTP, and DNS helps sysadmins troubleshoot connectivity issues and optimize network performance. They also work with cloud platforms, virtualization technologies like VMware and Hyper-V, and storage solutions to ensure that IT environments are scalable and resilient. System administrators play a crucial role in business continuity by maintaining disaster recovery plans, configuring failover mechanisms, and ensuring data integrity through backup solutions.

Automation is an essential aspect of modern system administration. Manually configuring servers and performing routine maintenance tasks can be time-consuming and prone to errors. Scripting languages such as Bash, PowerShell, and Python help sysadmins automate repetitive tasks, such as user provisioning, software installations, and log analysis. Configuration management tools like Ansible, Puppet, and Chef further enhance automation by allowing system administrators to define infrastructure as code (IaC), ensuring that system configurations are consistent across multiple servers. Mastering automation techniques improves efficiency, reduces downtime, and enhances system reliability.

As IT environments become more complex, organizations are increasingly adopting DevOps practices to improve software development and deployment processes. DevOps is a methodology that promotes collaboration between development and operations teams, emphasizing automation, continuous integration, and continuous deployment (CI/CD). By integrating DevOps principles, organizations can deliver software updates faster, maintain stable infrastructure, and enhance overall system performance. DevOps engineers work with tools such as Jenkins, Git, Docker, and Kubernetes to streamline development pipelines, automate testing, and manage containerized applications.

One of the core principles of DevOps is continuous integration and continuous deployment (CI/CD). CI/CD practices allow developers to frequently integrate code changes, automatically test software, and deploy applications with minimal manual intervention. Tools like Jenkins, GitLab CI/CD, and CircleCI help automate these processes, ensuring that software updates are thoroughly tested and deployed efficiently. Implementing CI/CD reduces the risk of software failures, shortens release cycles, and improves collaboration between development and operations teams. IT professionals interested in DevOps should familiarize themselves with CI/CD workflows and best practices to improve software delivery.

Containerization and orchestration are also fundamental concepts in DevOps. Traditional system administration relied on managing applications directly on physical servers or virtual machines, but containerization provides a more efficient way to deploy applications.

Containers encapsulate applications and their dependencies, ensuring consistency across different environments. Docker is one of the most widely used containerization tools, allowing developers and sysadmins to create, manage, and deploy containerized applications. Kubernetes, an orchestration platform, automates the deployment, scaling, and management of containers, making it easier to run applications in distributed environments. Learning how to use Docker and Kubernetes is essential for IT professionals interested in modern infrastructure management.

Monitoring and logging are crucial for both system administration and DevOps. IT professionals must ensure that systems remain operational and that performance issues are detected before they cause disruptions. Monitoring tools like Prometheus, Grafana, Nagios, and Zabbix provide real-time insights into server health, resource usage, and network traffic. Log management solutions such as ELK Stack (Elasticsearch, Logstash, Kibana) and Splunk help collect and analyze system logs, making it easier to troubleshoot errors and security incidents. Implementing proper monitoring and logging strategies enhances system visibility, reduces downtime, and improves overall system reliability.

Security is a critical aspect of system administration and DevOps. Protecting IT infrastructure from cyber threats requires implementing security best practices, such as enforcing strong authentication mechanisms, applying software patches, and configuring firewalls. DevOps security, often referred to as DevSecOps, integrates security into the software development lifecycle, ensuring that applications are built with security in mind. Security automation tools, such as HashiCorp Vault for secret management and AWS Security Hub for cloud security monitoring, help organizations detect vulnerabilities and enforce compliance. IT professionals should prioritize security by following industry standards and staying updated on emerging threats.

Cloud computing has transformed the way IT infrastructure is managed, making it essential for system administrators and DevOps engineers to understand cloud platforms such as Amazon Web Services (AWS), Microsoft Azure, and Google Cloud. Cloud computing provides scalable, on-demand resources, allowing organizations to deploy applications and infrastructure more efficiently. Cloud-native technologies, such as serverless computing and managed database services, further enhance system performance and reduce operational overhead. Learning cloud fundamentals, including infrastructure as a service (IaaS) and platform as a service (PaaS), helps IT professionals stay competitive in modern IT environments.

Developing a career in system administration or DevOps requires continuous learning and hands-on experience. Setting up a home lab, experimenting with cloud environments, and working on real-world projects provide valuable insights into managing IT infrastructure. Many professionals start with certifications such as CompTIA Linux+, RHCSA (Red Hat Certified System Administrator), AWS Certified SysOps Administrator, or Docker Certified Associate to validate their expertise. Engaging with IT communities, attending DevOps meetups, and contributing to open-source projects help professionals expand their knowledge and network with industry experts.

As technology evolves, the roles of system administrators and DevOps engineers continue to expand. Organizations are increasingly adopting automation, cloud computing, and DevOps practices to improve efficiency and scalability. IT professionals who invest in learning infrastructure automation, cloud technologies, and CI/CD pipelines position themselves for high-demand roles in modern IT environments. Mastering both system administration and DevOps principles enables professionals to build resilient, secure, and efficient IT infrastructures that support business growth and innovation.

Introduction to Ethical Hacking and Cybersecurity Careers

Cybersecurity has become one of the most critical fields in IT, protecting businesses, governments, and individuals from cyber threats that continue to grow in complexity. With the increasing reliance on digital systems, the demand for cybersecurity professionals has surged, offering numerous career opportunities for those interested in defending networks, applications, and data from attacks. Ethical hacking, a specialized field within cybersecurity, focuses on identifying vulnerabilities before malicious hackers can exploit them. Understanding cybersecurity fundamentals and exploring ethical hacking as a career path provides IT professionals with valuable skills and numerous job prospects.

Ethical hacking, also known as penetration testing or white-hat hacking, involves legally testing systems for security weaknesses. Ethical hackers use the same techniques as malicious attackers but with permission from organizations to strengthen their defenses. Their role is to simulate cyberattacks, identify vulnerabilities, and recommend security measures to prevent breaches. Ethical hackers help businesses protect sensitive information, comply with security regulations, and reduce the risk of cyber threats. By thinking like an attacker, they enhance security by proactively addressing weaknesses before real attackers can exploit them.

Cybersecurity careers extend beyond ethical hacking, covering areas such as network security, cloud security, digital forensics, threat intelligence, and security operations. Security analysts monitor network traffic for suspicious activities, responding to incidents and mitigating risks. Penetration testers conduct controlled attacks on systems to uncover vulnerabilities. Security engineers design and implement security measures to protect IT infrastructure. Incident responders investigate cyberattacks and develop strategies to prevent future incidents. Cybersecurity consultants advise businesses on security best practices, ensuring that their defenses are robust and compliant with industry standards.

One of the first steps in pursuing a cybersecurity career is understanding fundamental security concepts. Cyber threats come in many forms, including malware, phishing, ransomware, denial-of-service attacks, and social engineering. Security professionals must be familiar with these threats and understand how attackers exploit system weaknesses. Learning about encryption, authentication mechanisms, firewalls, intrusion detection systems, and access controls is essential for building a strong security foundation. Many cybersecurity professionals start by gaining hands-on experience with security tools and practicing in controlled environments.

Ethical hackers rely on a variety of tools and techniques to conduct penetration tests and assess security risks. Tools like Nmap help scan networks for open ports and vulnerabilities. Metasploit allows ethical hackers to simulate exploits and test system defenses. Burp Suite is used for web application security testing, identifying weaknesses such as SQL injection and cross-site scripting (XSS). Wireshark analyzes network traffic, detecting anomalies that could indicate security threats. Mastering these tools enables ethical hackers to conduct thorough security assessments and help organizations improve their security posture.

Certifications play a significant role in cybersecurity careers, validating skills and increasing job market competitiveness. The Certified Ethical Hacker (CEH) certification provides foundational knowledge of penetration testing techniques and ethical hacking methodologies. CompTIA Security+ covers security fundamentals, including risk management, cryptography, and network security. The Offensive Security Certified Professional (OSCP) certification is highly regarded for its hands-on penetration testing exam, requiring candidates to exploit vulnerabilities in a controlled environment. Other certifications, such as CISSP (Certified Information Systems Security Professional) and GIAC certifications, focus on advanced security management and specialized cybersecurity domains.

Practical experience is crucial for anyone looking to enter the cybersecurity field. Many aspiring ethical hackers participate in Capture The Flag (CTF) competitions, which provide hands-on challenges that test problem-solving skills in real-world hacking scenarios. Platforms like TryHackMe and Hack The Box offer interactive labs where individuals can practice penetration testing techniques in a safe environment. Setting up a home lab using virtual machines and security tools allows cybersecurity enthusiasts to experiment with different attack and defense strategies. Practical experience not only strengthens technical skills but also demonstrates a candidate's passion and commitment to cybersecurity.

Understanding cybersecurity laws and ethics is essential for ethical hackers and security professionals. Engaging in hacking activities without permission is illegal and can lead to severe consequences. Ethical hackers operate within legal boundaries, obtaining explicit authorization before conducting security tests. Security professionals must also adhere to industry standards and compliance regulations, such as GDPR, HIPAA, and PCI-DSS, which govern data protection and security practices. Maintaining ethical integrity is crucial for building a trustworthy reputation in the cybersecurity community.

Cybersecurity professionals must stay updated with the latest threats, vulnerabilities, and security technologies. Cybercriminals continuously develop new attack methods, requiring security experts to adapt and enhance their defenses. Following cybersecurity news, reading security blogs, and participating in online communities help professionals stay informed about emerging threats. Organizations such as OWASP (Open Web Application Security Project) provide valuable resources on web security best practices. Engaging with the cybersecurity community through forums, conferences, and industry events helps professionals exchange knowledge and learn from experienced security experts.

The cybersecurity job market offers diverse opportunities across different industries. Financial institutions, healthcare organizations, government agencies, and technology companies all require cybersecurity professionals to protect their systems and data. Many cybersecurity roles offer remote work options, allowing professionals to work for global organizations from anywhere. Entry-level positions, such as security analyst or junior penetration tester, provide a starting point for career growth. As professionals gain experience, they can advance to roles such as security architect, cybersecurity manager, or chief information security officer (CISO), leading security initiatives for organizations.

Soft skills are just as important as technical skills in cybersecurity careers. Security professionals often need to explain complex technical issues to non-technical stakeholders, making strong communication skills essential. Problem-solving and analytical thinking help security experts identify vulnerabilities and develop effective mitigation strategies. Attention to detail is crucial when analyzing security logs, conducting forensic investigations, and reviewing system configurations. Collaboration with IT teams, developers, and business leaders ensures that security measures align with organizational goals.

Developing both technical expertise and soft skills enhances a cybersecurity professional's effectiveness in the field.

Cybersecurity professionals must adopt a mindset of continuous learning, as the industry evolves rapidly. Cyber threats, attack techniques, and security technologies change constantly, requiring security experts to stay ahead of attackers. Taking advanced training courses, earning new certifications, and experimenting with emerging security tools help professionals remain competitive. Many cybersecurity specialists contribute to open-source security projects, conduct independent research, or write security blogs to share their knowledge with the community. A commitment to lifelong learning is essential for success in the cybersecurity industry.

Ethical hacking and cybersecurity careers offer exciting challenges and opportunities for those passionate about protecting digital systems. Learning security fundamentals, gaining hands-on experience, obtaining certifications, and staying informed about the latest threats are essential steps toward a successful career in cybersecurity. Whether working as a penetration tester, security analyst, or security engineer, professionals in this field play a crucial role in defending organizations from cyber threats and ensuring a safer digital world.

How to Get Into Data Science and AI from Zero

Data science and artificial intelligence have become two of the most in-demand fields in technology, offering exciting opportunities for those who enjoy working with data, developing machine learning models, and solving complex problems. Many people believe that breaking into these fields requires an advanced degree in mathematics or computer science, but with the right learning path, anyone can start from zero and build a career in data science and AI. Understanding the fundamental concepts, gaining practical experience, and developing problem-solving skills are the keys to success.

The first step in learning data science is understanding what it involves. Data science is the process of extracting meaningful insights from raw data using statistics, programming, and machine learning techniques. It involves collecting data, cleaning and preprocessing it, analyzing trends, building predictive models, and communicating findings. Artificial intelligence, on the other hand, focuses on creating systems that can simulate human intelligence. AI includes areas such as machine learning, deep learning, natural language processing, and computer vision. Both fields rely heavily on data and mathematical principles to build intelligent applications that improve decision-making and automate tasks.

A strong foundation in mathematics and statistics is essential for understanding data science and AI. Key concepts include probability, linear algebra, calculus, and statistical analysis. Probability helps in understanding randomness and uncertainty in data. Linear algebra is crucial for machine learning algorithms that use matrices and vectors. Calculus is used to optimize models and adjust learning parameters. Statistics allows data scientists to interpret patterns, test hypotheses, and make data-driven predictions. While advanced mathematical knowledge is not required initially, grasping these fundamental concepts will make it easier to learn machine learning and AI techniques.

Programming is another critical skill for entering data science and AI. Python is the most widely used programming language in this field due to its simplicity and powerful libraries. Beginners should start by learning Python basics, including variables, loops, functions, and data structures. Once comfortable with Python, it is important to explore data science libraries such as NumPy for numerical computing, Pandas for data manipulation, and Matplotlib or Seaborn for data visualization. These tools allow data scientists to clean, explore, and visualize data efficiently. Understanding how to write efficient code and work with data structures is a crucial step in the learning process.

Working with databases and big data technologies is also an important part of data science. SQL is the primary language for querying and managing structured data in relational databases. Learning how to write SQL queries, join tables, and optimize database performance helps in handling large datasets efficiently. For big data processing, tools like Apache Spark and Hadoop allow data scientists to analyze massive amounts of information distributed across multiple servers. Cloud platforms such as AWS, Google Cloud, and Azure provide scalable solutions for storing and processing data, making them valuable skills to learn for modern data science applications.

Exploring machine learning concepts is the next step in building expertise in data science and AI. Machine learning is a subset of AI that enables computers to learn patterns from data and make predictions without being explicitly programmed. Beginners should start by understanding supervised and unsupervised learning techniques. Supervised learning involves training models on labeled data to predict outcomes, while unsupervised learning finds hidden patterns in data without predefined labels. Popular machine learning algorithms include linear regression, decision trees, support vector machines, and clustering techniques like k-means.

Python libraries such as Scikit-learn provide easy-to-use tools for implementing machine learning models. Learning how to preprocess data, select appropriate features, train models, and evaluate performance is essential for building effective machine learning solutions. Hands-on projects, such as predicting house prices, detecting spam emails, or classifying images, reinforce theoretical knowledge and improve practical skills. Experimenting with different models and tuning hyperparameters helps in understanding how machine learning algorithms work in real-world scenarios.

Deep learning is an advanced area of AI that focuses on neural networks, which are computational models inspired by the human brain. Deep learning enables breakthroughs in fields such as image recognition, natural language processing, and autonomous systems. Popular deep learning frameworks include TensorFlow and PyTorch, which allow developers to build and train neural networks for complex tasks. Convolutional neural networks (CNNs) are used for image processing, recurrent neural networks (RNNs) for sequential data like speech recognition, and transformers for advanced natural language understanding. Learning how to use these tools opens up opportunities in cutting-edge AI applications.

Data science and AI are practical fields that require real-world experience to master. Working on hands-on projects is the best way to develop skills and build a portfolio. Beginners should start by analyzing publicly available datasets from platforms like Kaggle, which hosts competitions and datasets for experimentation. Projects such as predicting customer churn, sentiment analysis on social media data, and fraud detection provide valuable experience in handling real-world problems. Writing about projects, sharing findings, and documenting code on GitHub or personal blogs showcases skills to potential employers.

Understanding the ethical implications of data science and AI is crucial for responsible development. Issues such as bias in machine learning models, data privacy concerns, and the impact of AI on jobs require careful consideration. Data scientists must ensure that their models are fair, transparent, and do not reinforce harmful biases. Ethical AI principles emphasize accountability, inclusivity, and the responsible use of technology to benefit society. Learning about frameworks for ethical AI, such as explainable AI (XAI) and fairness-aware machine learning, helps in developing responsible AI solutions.

Networking and engaging with the data science and AI community accelerate learning and career growth. Joining online forums, attending meetups, participating in hackathons, and connecting with professionals on LinkedIn provide valuable opportunities to learn from experts and gain insights into industry trends. Platforms such as Towards Data Science, DataCamp, and Coursera offer educational resources and practical tutorials. Engaging with the community allows aspiring data scientists to stay updated on new research, job opportunities, and best practices in the field.

Certifications and advanced education help validate skills and enhance career prospects in data science and AI. While a formal degree is not always required, earning certifications such as Google TensorFlow Developer, IBM Data Science Professional, or AWS Machine Learning Specialty can boost credibility. Many universities and online platforms offer specialized courses in machine learning, deep learning, and AI, providing structured learning paths for career advancement. Continuous learning is essential in this field, as new algorithms, frameworks, and methodologies are constantly being developed.

Breaking into data science and AI from zero requires dedication, curiosity, and hands-on practice. By building a strong foundation in mathematics, programming, machine learning, and data analysis, aspiring professionals can develop the skills needed to succeed in this rapidly growing industry. Engaging in real-world projects, learning from industry experts, and staying committed to continuous improvement open doors to exciting career opportunities in data science and AI.

The Role of Open Source in IT Careers

Open source has played a transformative role in the IT industry, shaping the way software is developed, distributed, and maintained. Unlike proprietary software, open-source projects make their source code freely available for anyone to view, modify, and contribute to. This model fosters collaboration, innovation, and accessibility, making it an essential part of modern IT careers. For professionals entering the field, engaging with open-source software provides invaluable hands-on experience, career growth opportunities, and the ability to contribute to widely used technologies. Understanding how open source influences IT careers can help professionals make strategic decisions about learning, networking, and professional development.

One of the greatest benefits of open source is its accessibility. Many of the most widely used technologies in IT are open source, including operating systems like Linux, programming languages like Python, frameworks like React and Django, and infrastructure tools like Kubernetes and Docker. Because open-source software is freely available, IT professionals can experiment with and learn from real-world codebases without the limitations of expensive proprietary software. This accessibility makes open source an excellent starting point for beginners, as they can study existing projects, modify code, and build their own applications using established frameworks and libraries.

Open source also provides IT professionals with opportunities to gain hands-on experience. Many aspiring developers, system administrators, and cybersecurity professionals start their careers by contributing to open-source projects. By fixing bugs, adding new features, or improving documentation, contributors gain practical experience that can be added to their resumes. Employers highly value candidates who have real-world coding experience, and contributing to open-source projects demonstrates technical proficiency, problem-solving abilities, and collaboration skills. Unlike academic or personal projects, contributions to well-known open-source projects provide verifiable proof of a candidate's abilities.

Collaboration is a core principle of open-source development. Many open-source projects are maintained by distributed teams of developers, security experts, and IT professionals from around the world. Contributors work together through version control systems like Git and platforms like GitHub, GitLab, and Bitbucket. Learning how to use Git for collaboration is an essential skill in modern IT careers, as it is widely used in professional software development and system administration. Through pull requests, code reviews, and discussions, contributors refine their coding skills, receive feedback from experienced developers, and learn industry best practices.

Networking is another major advantage of participating in open-source projects. Many IT professionals build strong relationships with other contributors, project maintainers, and industry leaders through their open-source work. These connections can lead to job opportunities, mentorship, and collaboration on future projects. Many companies actively recruit developers and engineers who have contributed to open-source projects, as it demonstrates initiative, technical expertise, and the ability to work in a team environment. Attending open-source conferences, participating in hackathons, and engaging in online communities further strengthens professional networks.

For system administrators and DevOps engineers, open-source tools are a fundamental part of managing infrastructure and automating processes. Technologies such as Ansible, Terraform, and Prometheus are widely used for configuration management, infrastructure as code, and monitoring. Learning how to deploy, configure, and troubleshoot these tools prepares IT professionals for roles in cloud computing, system administration, and DevOps. Many organizations prefer open-source solutions over proprietary software due to their flexibility, cost-effectiveness, and strong community support. Becoming proficient in these tools increases job market competitiveness and career advancement opportunities.

Cybersecurity professionals also benefit from open-source resources. Many security tools, such as Metasploit for penetration testing, Wireshark for network analysis, and OSSEC for intrusion detection, are open source. Ethical hackers and security analysts use these tools to test system defenses, investigate security incidents, and analyze vulnerabilities. Open-source security research helps the industry stay ahead of cyber threats by sharing knowledge, developing new techniques, and improving existing security tools. Professionals who contribute to open-source security projects gain credibility in the cybersecurity community and can showcase their expertise to potential employers.

The open-source model also encourages innovation by allowing developers to experiment with new ideas and collaborate on groundbreaking technologies. Many of today's leading tech companies, including Google, Microsoft, and Facebook, actively contribute to open-source projects and release their own technologies as open source. Frameworks like TensorFlow for machine learning, Kubernetes for container orchestration, and Chromium for web browsers have all been developed as open-source projects. IT professionals who engage with these projects gain insights into cutting-edge technologies and can contribute to their development, positioning themselves at the forefront of industry advancements.

Documentation and technical writing are important aspects of open-source contributions. Many projects rely on clear, well-structured documentation to help users and contributors understand how to use and extend the software. Writing tutorials, improving README files, and creating user guides provide valuable experience in technical communication. Many IT professionals, including developers, system administrators, and security analysts, are expected to write clear documentation in their jobs. Contributing to open-source documentation not only helps the community but also strengthens a contributor's ability to explain technical concepts effectively.

For those looking to transition into IT careers, open-source contributions provide a practical way to build a portfolio. Many hiring managers look for real-world experience, and showcasing open-source projects on a resume or GitHub profile helps demonstrate technical skills. Job seekers who lack formal work experience can use open-source projects as proof of their capabilities. By working on real-world codebases, contributors learn how to navigate large projects, follow best practices, and collaborate with teams, all of which are essential skills in professional IT roles.

The open-source movement is also shaping the future of education and skills development. Many universities and coding bootcamps incorporate open-source projects into their curricula, allowing students to gain practical experience while contributing to meaningful software development. Free and open-source platforms like freeCodeCamp, The Odin Project, and Mozilla Developer Network provide learning resources for aspiring IT professionals. The open-source philosophy of knowledge sharing and accessibility makes high-quality technical education available to anyone with an internet connection.

As IT continues to evolve, the role of open source will only grow in importance. Many companies are shifting towards open-source software for its cost savings, transparency, and flexibility. Governments and organizations around the world are adopting open standards and promoting open-source collaboration. IT professionals who understand how to leverage open-source technologies, contribute to projects, and engage with the community will have a strong advantage in their careers.

Engaging with open-source software provides a wealth of opportunities for IT professionals at all levels. Whether through coding, documentation, security research, or infrastructure management, contributing to open-source projects builds practical experience, strengthens problem-solving skills, and connects professionals with a global network of peers. Open source is more than just a way to develop software—it is a pathway to career growth, innovation, and professional development in the ever-expanding world of IT.

Learning IT from Real-World Case Studies

One of the most effective ways to learn IT is by studying real-world case studies that highlight how technology is applied to solve complex problems. Unlike theoretical knowledge, which provides foundational principles, case studies offer practical insights into how IT professionals tackle challenges, optimize systems, and implement innovative solutions. Examining real-world scenarios allows learners to understand the decision-making process, evaluate different approaches, and apply problem-solving skills in real IT environments. Case studies serve as valuable learning tools for aspiring IT professionals, providing a bridge between academic knowledge and practical experience.

One of the most well-known case studies in IT revolves around the migration of companies from traditional on-premises infrastructure to cloud computing. Organizations such as Netflix, Airbnb, and Spotify successfully transitioned to cloud platforms like Amazon Web Services (AWS) to improve scalability, reliability, and cost efficiency. The decision to move to the cloud required careful planning, risk assessment, and execution. By studying these cases, IT learners can understand the challenges of cloud adoption, such as data migration, security considerations, and performance optimization. These real-world examples highlight the importance of cloud computing skills, making it clear why companies prioritize professionals with expertise in cloud services.

Cybersecurity breaches provide another set of real-world case studies that help IT professionals understand security risks and mitigation strategies. High-profile incidents such as the Equifax data breach, the WannaCry ransomware attack, and the SolarWinds supply chain attack illustrate how cybercriminals exploit vulnerabilities to gain unauthorized access to sensitive data. Analyzing these cases helps learners understand the importance of encryption, network security, incident response, and security best practices. IT professionals studying these breaches can see how security flaws were exploited, what countermeasures were taken, and how organizations improved their cybersecurity posture after the incidents.

System failures and outages also serve as valuable case studies for IT learners. Large-scale service disruptions, such as the global Facebook outage or airline IT system failures, highlight the critical role of infrastructure reliability and disaster recovery planning. These cases demonstrate the impact of downtime on businesses and users, emphasizing the need for high availability, redundancy, and failover mechanisms. Learning from these incidents helps IT professionals understand how to design resilient systems, implement load balancing, and develop effective backup strategies to minimize disruptions.

Software development projects provide another category of real-world case studies that showcase the challenges of building and maintaining applications. The development of open-source projects such as the Linux operating system or the Apache web server illustrates the power of community-driven software development. Conversely, failed software projects, such as the healthcare.gov launch or Microsoft's Windows Vista, reveal how poor project management, lack of user testing, and misalignment between stakeholders can lead to failures. By analyzing successful and unsuccessful software projects, IT learners gain insights into agile development, software testing, and the importance of user experience.

Network infrastructure failures offer valuable lessons in IT networking and system administration. Case studies such as the global DNS outage that disrupted major websites or large-scale Distributed Denial of Service (DDoS) attacks highlight the importance of robust networking practices. IT professionals studying these cases can understand how misconfigurations, lack of redundancy, and outdated security protocols contribute to network failures. These examples reinforce the need for proper network segmentation, firewall configurations, and proactive monitoring to prevent and mitigate network disruptions.

Automation and DevOps transformation provide another source of real-world IT case studies. Companies that successfully implemented DevOps practices, such as Google, Amazon, and Microsoft, showcase how automation, continuous integration, and continuous deployment (CI/CD) improve software delivery. These cases illustrate the benefits of infrastructure as code, containerization, and automated testing in modern IT operations. Learning from these examples helps IT professionals understand how to implement automation frameworks, optimize workflows, and enhance collaboration between development and operations teams.

Data science and artificial intelligence case studies highlight the power of data-driven decision-making. Companies like Google and Facebook use AI to personalize content, improve search algorithms, and enhance user experiences. The use of AI in fraud detection, medical diagnostics, and predictive analytics demonstrates the practical applications of machine learning. Studying real-world AI projects helps learners understand the challenges of training models, handling large datasets, and addressing biases in AI systems. These cases also emphasize the importance of ethical considerations when deploying AI solutions.

IT support and troubleshooting case studies reveal the real-world challenges faced by IT professionals in help desk and technical support roles. Examining cases where IT teams had to diagnose and resolve critical issues, such as hardware failures, software bugs, or misconfigurations, helps learners develop problem-solving skills. These case studies highlight the importance of logical troubleshooting, customer communication, and documentation. Understanding how IT teams handle real support scenarios prepares learners for practical challenges in their careers.

Enterprise IT transformations provide another rich source of case studies. Many large organizations have modernized their IT infrastructure by transitioning from legacy systems to modern architectures. The adoption of microservices, hybrid cloud solutions, and artificial intelligence-powered automation illustrates how businesses leverage technology to stay competitive. Studying these transitions helps IT professionals understand the complexities of system integration, change management, and digital transformation strategies. These case studies highlight the importance of IT leadership, strategic planning, and adaptability in a rapidly evolving industry.

Open-source contributions and community-driven software development also provide valuable learning opportunities. Many IT professionals have gained experience and recognition by contributing to open-source projects such as Kubernetes, TensorFlow, and WordPress. Studying how these projects are structured, managed, and maintained gives learners a deeper understanding of collaborative software development. IT professionals who engage with open-source projects not only build their technical skills but also expand their professional networks.

By analyzing real-world IT case studies, professionals can bridge the gap between theory and practice. These case studies provide practical insights into troubleshooting, system design, security best practices, and software development methodologies. They offer valuable lessons in risk management, decision-making, and critical thinking, preparing IT professionals for real challenges they will encounter in their careers. Through continuous learning and analysis of real-world scenarios, aspiring IT professionals can develop a problem-solving mindset and gain the experience needed to succeed in the ever-evolving world of technology.

Choosing Your Next IT Certification After the First One

Earning the first IT certification is an important milestone, providing foundational knowledge and validating technical skills. However, the journey does not stop there. The IT industry is highly dynamic, and professionals need to continuously update their skills to stay competitive. Choosing the next certification strategically can open new career opportunities, increase earning potential, and deepen expertise in a specific field. With numerous certification paths available, it is essential to select one that aligns with career goals, industry demand, and areas of interest.

The first step in deciding on the next certification is evaluating career objectives. IT covers many disciplines, including networking, cybersecurity, cloud computing, system administration, data science, and software development. Professionals should consider whether they want to specialize in their current field, expand into a related domain, or switch to a new area of expertise. For example, someone who has earned CompTIA A+ might choose to move into networking with CompTIA Network+ or explore cybersecurity with CompTIA Security+.

Identifying a clear career path helps in selecting a certification that provides relevant and valuable skills.

Understanding industry demand is another important factor. Certain certifications are highly sought after by employers and can significantly improve job prospects. Researching job postings, speaking with IT professionals, and reviewing industry reports help determine which certifications offer the best return on investment. Certifications in cybersecurity, cloud computing, and DevOps are particularly valuable due to the increasing reliance on secure and scalable IT solutions. If a professional is unsure about their next step, looking at in-demand certifications in their field can provide useful guidance.

Building upon existing knowledge is a common approach when selecting the next certification. Many certifications follow a structured path, allowing professionals to advance from beginner to expert levels. For example, someone who has earned Cisco's CCNA might pursue CCNP to gain deeper networking expertise. A cybersecurity professional with CompTIA Security+ might choose Certified Ethical Hacker (CEH) or CISSP to specialize further. Following a logical progression ensures that each certification builds upon previously acquired skills, making learning more effective and preparing for more complex job roles.

Exploring vendor-specific versus vendor-neutral certifications is another key consideration. Vendor-neutral certifications, such as CompTIA, ISACA, and EC-Council certifications, provide broad knowledge applicable to multiple environments. These certifications are beneficial for professionals who work with various technologies and do not want to be limited to a specific vendor. On the other hand, vendor-specific certifications, such as those from Microsoft, AWS, Cisco, or Google, focus on particular platforms and tools. These certifications are ideal for professionals who work with or plan to specialize in a vendor's ecosystem. Choosing between vendor-neutral and vendor-specific certifications depends on career goals and job market needs.

For professionals in networking, the next certification often depends on their existing credentials. Those with CompTIA Network+ may consider Cisco's CCNA for a deeper understanding of networking technologies. For more advanced networking knowledge, CCNP or Juniper JNCIA offer specialized learning paths. Network engineers who want to focus on security can transition to cybersecurity certifications such as Cisco's CCNP Security or Palo Alto Networks PCNSA. Each step in the certification path increases expertise and prepares professionals for higher-level responsibilities in networking and security.

Cybersecurity is one of the fastest-growing IT fields, with multiple certification paths available. After earning an entry-level certification like CompTIA Security+, professionals may choose CEH for penetration testing, CISSP for security management, or GIAC certifications for specialized areas like incident response or digital forensics. Cybersecurity professionals must also consider certifications that align with regulatory compliance, such as CISM or CISA, which focus on security governance and auditing. Given the increasing number of cyber threats, earning multiple cybersecurity certifications can enhance job opportunities and salary potential.

Cloud computing certifications are valuable for professionals working in IT infrastructure, system administration, and DevOps. After earning a foundational cloud certification, such as AWS Certified Cloud Practitioner or Microsoft Azure Fundamentals, professionals can advance to AWS Solutions Architect Associate, Azure Administrator Associate, or Google Cloud Associate Engineer. More advanced cloud certifications, such as AWS Solutions Architect Professional or Google Cloud Professional Cloud Architect, focus on designing and managing large-scale cloud infrastructures. Cloud security certifications, like AWS Security Specialty or Azure Security Engineer, are ideal for professionals who want to specialize in securing cloud environments.

For those in system administration, certifications help expand knowledge and open career advancement opportunities. After earning CompTIA Linux+ or LPIC-1, professionals can pursue LPIC-2 for more advanced Linux administration. Microsoft Certified: Azure Administrator Associate is ideal for Windows system administrators transitioning to cloud environments. Certifications like Red Hat Certified Engineer (RHCE) validate expertise in enterprise Linux environments. System administrators interested in automation and DevOps can explore certifications such as Terraform Associate or

Kubernetes Certified Administrator (CKA) to gain skills in infrastructure as code and container orchestration.

Software development professionals have a variety of certification options depending on their specialization. Microsoft Certified: Azure Developer Associate is beneficial for those developing cloud applications. Google Professional Data Engineer is useful for software engineers working with data science and AI. Java, Python, and Microsoft certifications validate programming expertise and demonstrate proficiency in specific languages. Developers interested in security can pursue certifications such as CSSLP to learn about secure coding practices. Advanced certifications, such as Google TensorFlow Developer, allow AI engineers to showcase expertise in machine learning frameworks.

Data science and AI certifications are growing in popularity as more businesses adopt data-driven strategies. Professionals who start with entry-level data certifications, such as IBM Data Science Professional Certificate or Microsoft Certified: Azure Data Scientist Associate, can advance to more specialized credentials like Google Professional Machine Learning Engineer or AWS Certified Machine Learning Specialty. Certifications in big data, such as Cloudera Certified Data Engineer or Databricks Certified Data Analyst, help professionals build expertise in large-scale data processing. Choosing a data science certification depends on career goals and the technologies used in an organization.

Project management certifications are valuable for IT professionals looking to move into leadership roles. IT professionals with technical expertise may choose to pursue PMP (Project Management Professional) or PRINCE2 to enhance their ability to manage IT projects. Agile certifications, such as Certified Scrum Master (CSM) or PMI-ACP, focus on managing projects using agile methodologies. ITIL certifications help IT professionals optimize service management and improve IT operations. These certifications complement technical skills and prepare professionals for managerial positions in IT departments.

Selecting the right certification requires careful planning, but the effort pays off in career growth and new opportunities. IT professionals should consider factors such as career goals, industry demand, vendor preferences, and specialization areas when choosing their next certification. Investing in continuous learning through certifications ensures that professionals remain competitive, expand their expertise, and advance their careers in the ever-evolving IT industry.

Building a Personal Brand in IT

In the competitive world of IT, technical skills alone are not always enough to stand out. Building a personal brand is essential for establishing credibility, showcasing expertise, and opening new career opportunities. A strong personal brand helps IT professionals differentiate themselves, attract job offers, and gain recognition in the industry. Whether pursuing a career in software development, cybersecurity, cloud computing, or data science, creating a professional identity allows individuals to demonstrate their value, share their knowledge, and build meaningful connections.

The first step in building a personal brand is defining a niche or area of specialization. IT is a broad field, and professionals who establish themselves as experts in a particular domain gain more visibility and credibility. Choosing a niche that aligns with interests, skills, and career goals helps create a clear and consistent professional identity. Whether specializing in ethical hacking, cloud architecture, DevOps, AI, or network security, focusing on a specific area enables IT professionals to position themselves as authorities in their chosen field. A well-defined niche makes it easier to develop content, contribute to discussions, and attract the right audience.

Creating an online presence is crucial for building a personal brand in IT. A professional LinkedIn profile serves as a digital resume, showcasing skills, certifications, and work experience. Optimizing a LinkedIn profile with a well-written summary, detailed job descriptions, and relevant keywords improves visibility in search results and attracts recruiters. Regularly posting industry insights, sharing project updates, and engaging with other professionals on LinkedIn establishes credibility and demonstrates expertise. Participating in LinkedIn discussions, commenting on technical articles, and networking with industry leaders further enhances visibility and professional reputation.

A personal website or portfolio provides a centralized platform for showcasing technical skills and achievements. A well-designed website includes an about section, a resume, links to projects, blog posts, and contact information. Developers can share GitHub repositories, data scientists can display interactive visualizations, and cybersecurity professionals can document penetration testing techniques. Writing technical articles and tutorials on a personal blog demonstrates thought leadership and helps others learn from experiences. A portfolio serves as a powerful tool for job applications, freelance opportunities, and collaborations by providing tangible proof of skills and accomplishments.

Contributing to open-source projects is an excellent way to build a personal brand while gaining hands-on experience. Open-source contributions allow IT professionals to work on real-world projects, collaborate with experienced developers, and improve coding skills. Platforms like GitHub, GitLab, and Bitbucket provide opportunities to contribute to software frameworks, automation tools, and security research. Open-source involvement showcases problem-solving abilities, teamwork, and a willingness to contribute to the IT community. Employers and recruiters often value candidates who actively participate in open-source projects, as it demonstrates technical competence and initiative.

Public speaking and attending industry events help IT professionals expand their reach and establish authority in their field. Presenting at conferences, webinars, or local meetups provides an opportunity to share knowledge, engage with the community, and build credibility. Topics can range from explaining a new programming language to discussing cybersecurity threats or cloud best practices. Even those who are not comfortable speaking publicly can participate in panel discussions, moderate technical forums, or host virtual study groups. Speaking engagements create lasting impressions and strengthen professional networks.

Engaging in social media platforms such as Twitter, Reddit, and Discord allows IT professionals to connect with industry peers, join discussions, and stay updated on emerging trends. Twitter is a valuable platform for sharing quick insights, participating in hashtag discussions, and following influential figures in IT. Reddit communities, such as r/learnprogramming and r/netsec, provide spaces for sharing knowledge, asking questions, and networking. Discord and Slack groups dedicated to IT fields offer real-time discussions, mentorship opportunities, and collaborative projects. Active participation in these communities enhances visibility and builds a strong personal brand.

Publishing content regularly establishes expertise and thought leadership in IT. Writing technical blog posts, creating video tutorials, or producing podcast episodes allows professionals to share their knowledge with a wider audience. Platforms like Medium, Dev.to, and YouTube provide spaces for publishing content and reaching IT enthusiasts worldwide. Tutorials on troubleshooting common issues, guides on configuring servers, or discussions about AI ethics showcase expertise and attract followers. Consistently producing valuable content helps build credibility, increase engagement, and create long-term professional opportunities.

Networking plays a critical role in personal branding by building relationships with other professionals, mentors, and potential employers. Attending networking events, participating in hackathons, and joining professional organizations provide opportunities to connect with like-minded individuals. Mentorship, both giving and receiving, enhances professional growth and strengthens connections in the industry. A well-established network increases the chances of learning about job openings, collaboration opportunities, and industry trends. Strong networking skills complement technical expertise and contribute to long-term career success.

Earning industry-recognized certifications reinforces a personal brand by validating skills and knowledge. Certifications such as AWS Certified Solutions Architect, Cisco CCNA, Certified Ethical Hacker (CEH), and Google Cloud Professional Engineer demonstrate expertise in specific areas. Displaying certification badges on LinkedIn profiles, personal websites, and resumes highlights professional achievements and credibility. Many IT professionals share their certification journey, study tips, and exam experiences online, helping others while showcasing their commitment to continuous learning. Certifications enhance reputation and increase job market competitiveness.

Staying active in IT communities and forums strengthens a personal brand by positioning professionals as reliable sources of knowledge. Answering technical questions on Stack Overflow, writing responses on Quora, or participating in cybersecurity discussions on forums like Hack The Box builds recognition. Helping others solve technical problems and sharing best practices demonstrates expertise and establishes a strong reputation. Consistently providing value to the community increases visibility and trust within the industry.

Maintaining authenticity is key to building a successful personal brand. IT professionals should focus on sharing genuine experiences, challenges, and successes rather than creating an artificial image. Transparency about learning journeys, mistakes made, and lessons learned resonates with others and fosters meaningful connections. Authenticity builds trust and credibility, making personal branding efforts more effective and sustainable. People are more likely to engage with and support professionals who are honest, approachable, and willing to share their knowledge.

Adapting and evolving the personal brand over time ensures continued relevance in the industry. As technology advances, professionals must stay updated with new skills, certifications, and industry developments. Revisiting and refining personal websites, updating LinkedIn profiles, and expanding content topics keep the personal brand aligned with career growth. Continuous learning and engagement in the IT community reinforce expertise and demonstrate a commitment to professional development. A strong personal brand evolves alongside industry trends, maintaining its value and impact over time.

Building a personal brand in IT requires consistency, engagement, and a willingness to share knowledge. Establishing an online presence, contributing to open-source projects, networking with industry professionals, and creating valuable content all contribute to a strong professional identity. A well-defined personal brand enhances career opportunities, attracts job offers, and positions IT professionals as trusted experts in their field. By strategically developing a personal brand, IT professionals can differentiate themselves and create lasting success in the ever-evolving technology landscape.

Exploring the Future of IT Careers

The IT industry is constantly evolving, driven by advancements in technology, automation, and digital transformation. As businesses, governments, and individuals continue to rely on technology, the demand for IT professionals continues to grow. Emerging technologies such as artificial intelligence, cloud computing, cybersecurity, blockchain, and quantum computing are shaping the future of IT careers. Professionals entering or already working in the field must adapt to these changes by continuously learning new skills and staying updated with industry trends. Understanding where IT careers are headed helps individuals make informed decisions about their professional development and long-term career prospects.

Artificial intelligence and machine learning are among the most influential technologies shaping the future of IT. AI is becoming increasingly integrated into business operations, healthcare, finance, cybersecurity, and automation. Companies are leveraging AI-powered tools for data analysis, fraud detection, customer support, and decision-making. Machine learning engineers, AI researchers, and data scientists are in high demand as organizations seek to harness the power of AI to improve efficiency and innovation. IT professionals who gain expertise in neural networks, deep learning, and natural language processing will have significant career opportunities as AI adoption continues to expand.

Cloud computing has transformed the IT industry by enabling businesses to scale infrastructure, reduce costs, and improve agility. Organizations are increasingly shifting from traditional on-premises systems to cloud-based environments using platforms like Amazon Web Services, Microsoft Azure, and Google Cloud. Cloud architects, DevOps engineers, and cloud security specialists are among the most sought-after roles in this domain. The ability to design, deploy, and manage cloud infrastructure is becoming an essential skill for IT professionals. As hybrid and multi-cloud strategies gain popularity, expertise in cloud automation, containerization, and serverless computing will be highly valuable.

Cybersecurity remains a critical aspect of IT careers as cyber threats continue to grow in complexity and frequency. With the rise of ransomware attacks, data breaches, and nation-state cyber warfare, businesses and governments are prioritizing cybersecurity investments. Cybersecurity analysts, ethical hackers, penetration testers, and security architects play essential roles in protecting digital assets. As regulations and compliance requirements evolve, professionals with expertise in cybersecurity frameworks, risk management, and threat intelligence will be in high demand. The future of cybersecurity careers will involve AI-driven threat detection, zero-trust security models, and enhanced encryption techniques.

Blockchain technology is no longer limited to cryptocurrencies; it is now being used in supply chain management, digital identity verification, and smart contracts. Decentralized applications and blockchain-based solutions are gaining traction across industries such as finance, healthcare, and logistics. IT professionals who understand blockchain development, cryptographic security, and decentralized finance will find new career opportunities in this expanding field. Companies are exploring blockchain for secure transactions, fraud prevention, and transparent record-keeping. As blockchain adoption increases, developers and architects specializing in distributed ledger technologies will play a crucial role in building next-generation digital systems.

Quantum computing is an emerging field that has the potential to revolutionize data processing and problem-solving capabilities. Unlike traditional computers that rely on binary processing, quantum computers use quantum bits (qubits) to perform calculations at unprecedented speeds. Industries such as pharmaceuticals, materials science, and finance are exploring quantum computing for complex simulations and optimization problems. Although quantum computing is still in its early stages, IT professionals interested in this field should focus on learning quantum algorithms, cryptography, and quantum programming languages such as Qiskit. As research and development in quantum computing progress, new career paths will emerge for those with expertise in this cutting-edge technology.

The rise of automation and robotic process automation (RPA) is reshaping IT roles by reducing repetitive tasks and increasing efficiency. Businesses are implementing RPA tools to streamline workflows, improve accuracy, and enhance productivity. IT professionals with knowledge of automation frameworks, scripting languages, and AI-driven automation will have a competitive advantage. System administrators and IT support specialists must adapt to working with automation tools that manage IT infrastructure, monitor system performance, and resolve technical issues without human intervention. Understanding how to integrate automation with existing IT processes will be a crucial skill in the future job market.

The Internet of Things (IoT) is expanding as more devices become connected to the internet, from smart home systems to industrial sensors. IoT engineers, embedded systems developers, and network specialists are needed to design and secure connected devices. With the growth of smart cities, healthcare monitoring systems, and industrial automation, professionals with expertise in IoT security, edge computing, and data analytics will find numerous career opportunities. As IoT adoption increases, the need for scalable networks, secure communication protocols, and efficient data processing will drive innovation in this field.

Remote work and the gig economy are influencing how IT professionals approach their careers. Many organizations have adopted hybrid or fully remote work models, allowing IT professionals to work from anywhere in the world. The rise of freelancing and contract work in IT provides opportunities for skilled professionals to work on diverse projects, from software development to cybersecurity consulting. Platforms like Upwork, Fiverr, and Toptal connect IT professionals with businesses looking for specialized skills. Remote work has also increased the demand for cloud-based collaboration tools, virtual private networks, and cybersecurity measures to protect remote work environments.

Soft skills such as problem-solving, communication, and adaptability are becoming increasingly important in IT careers. As technology evolves, IT professionals must be able to explain complex concepts to non-technical stakeholders, work in cross-functional teams, and manage projects effectively. Leadership and business acumen are valuable for IT professionals who aspire to management roles. Companies are seeking IT leaders who can align technology with business goals, drive digital transformation, and navigate the challenges of an ever-changing technological landscape. The ability to combine technical expertise with strategic thinking will be essential for long-term career growth.

Continuous learning is a fundamental requirement for IT professionals who want to stay ahead in the industry. Technology is evolving at a rapid pace, making it necessary to stay updated with new developments, certifications, and programming languages. Online learning platforms, coding bootcamps, and professional certifications provide opportunities for IT professionals to expand their skill sets. Organizations value employees who demonstrate a commitment to self-improvement and adaptability. Whether through formal education, industry certifications, or hands-on experience, continuous learning ensures that IT professionals remain competitive and relevant in the job market.

The future of IT careers is filled with exciting opportunities and challenges. Emerging technologies such as AI, cloud computing, cybersecurity, blockchain, quantum computing, and automation are shaping the industry in new ways. Professionals who invest in learning, adapt to technological advancements, and develop both technical and soft skills will thrive in this evolving landscape. By staying informed about industry trends and embracing lifelong learning, IT professionals can position themselves for success in the rapidly changing world of technology.

How to Negotiate Your First IT Salary

Negotiating a salary for the first IT job can feel intimidating, but it is an essential skill that helps ensure fair compensation for the work performed. Many entry-level IT professionals hesitate to negotiate, fearing they might lose the job offer or seem ungrateful. However, employers expect some level of negotiation, and those who advocate for themselves often secure better pay and benefits. Understanding how to research market rates, communicate effectively, and confidently discuss salary expectations can make a significant difference in financial and career growth.

The first step in salary negotiation is researching industry standards. Salaries in IT vary based on location, company size, job role, and experience level. Websites like Glassdoor, Payscale, and LinkedIn Salary Insights provide data on average salaries for different IT positions in various regions. Reviewing salary reports and talking to professionals in the industry can help establish a reasonable expectation for a given role. Knowing the average pay range for a specific position allows candidates to set realistic salary expectations and strengthens their negotiation position.

Understanding the full compensation package is equally important. Many IT jobs offer benefits beyond base salary, including bonuses, stock options, remote work flexibility, paid certifications, and professional development programs. Some companies provide tuition reimbursement, wellness programs, or additional vacation days. Before negotiating, it is helpful to consider which benefits matter most. For example, an entry-level IT professional who wants to advance quickly may prioritize paid training opportunities over a slightly higher salary. Evaluating the complete compensation package ensures that the final agreement aligns with career goals and personal needs.

Timing plays a critical role in salary negotiations. The best time to discuss salary is after receiving a job offer but before formally accepting it. Bringing up salary expectations too early in the interview process may reduce leverage, as the employer has not yet decided to hire the candidate. Waiting until after receiving an offer shifts the power dynamic, as the employer has already invested time and resources in the hiring process. At this stage, the company is more likely to negotiate rather than restart the hiring process with a new candidate.

Confidence and preparation are key when discussing salary. IT professionals should practice stating their salary expectations clearly and professionally. Instead of simply asking for a higher salary, providing justification based on research and skills strengthens the argument. For example, if the average salary for a network administrator in a particular city is $65,000 and the company offers $58,000, the candidate can highlight industry standards and relevant skills to support a counteroffer. Demonstrating the value that will be brought to the company increases the chances of a successful negotiation.

Framing the conversation positively helps maintain professionalism. Instead of demanding a higher salary, expressing enthusiasm for the role while discussing compensation expectations fosters a collaborative discussion. A statement such as "I'm excited about this opportunity and eager to contribute. Based on my research and the industry standard for this role, I was expecting something in the range of $65,000. Is there flexibility in the offer?" invites discussion rather than confrontation. Employers are more likely to negotiate when approached with a positive and constructive attitude.

IT professionals should also be prepared for different responses from employers. If an employer agrees to the request immediately, it confirms that negotiation was worthwhile. If the employer makes a counteroffer, evaluating whether it aligns with expectations is essential. In some cases, companies may have strict salary structures and may not offer much flexibility in base pay but may be open to adjusting benefits, signing bonuses, or additional perks. Being open to alternative forms of compensation can result in a better overall package.

Knowing when to accept an offer or walk away is an important aspect of salary negotiation. If a company is unwilling to meet salary expectations and the offer is significantly below market value, it may be worth reconsidering whether the role is the right fit. However, if the offer is competitive and aligns with career goals, accepting it and focusing on long-term growth can be a good strategy. Evaluating job satisfaction, career development opportunities, and workplace culture helps in making an informed decision beyond just salary.

For those who feel uncomfortable negotiating, practicing conversations with a friend, mentor, or career coach can build confidence. Role-playing different scenarios and responses to employer counteroffers helps develop effective negotiation skills. Writing down key points and rehearsing how to state salary expectations ensures a more structured and confident conversation. Many first-time job seekers underestimate their value, but practicing negotiation techniques helps overcome hesitation and builds self-assurance.

Salary negotiation is not just about the first job; it sets the foundation for future earnings. Accepting a lower salary early in a career can impact long-term earnings, as raises and promotions are often based on current pay. Advocating for fair compensation from the start helps establish a strong financial trajectory. IT professionals who negotiate effectively develop a valuable career skill that benefits them throughout their professional journey.

While negotiating salary can be challenging, it is a critical step in securing fair compensation for skills and expertise. Conducting thorough research, preparing a clear argument, and approaching the conversation with confidence and professionalism increase the chances of a successful outcome. Employers expect candidates to negotiate, and those who do so effectively demonstrate initiative and business awareness. By mastering the art of salary negotiation early in their careers, IT professionals set themselves up for financial success and long-term career growth.

Final Tips for a Successful IT Career Journey

Building a successful career in IT requires a combination of technical expertise, continuous learning, adaptability, and professional networking. The technology industry evolves rapidly, and those who remain proactive in their development will find greater opportunities for career growth and stability. Whether just starting out or already working in the field, following key strategies can make a significant difference in long-term success. Developing strong problem-solving skills, staying updated with industry trends, and maintaining a professional reputation are essential for navigating the competitive world of IT.

A mindset of continuous learning is one of the most valuable assets in an IT career. Technology does not remain static, and professionals who commit to ongoing education stay ahead of industry changes. New programming languages, frameworks, security threats, and cloud technologies emerge regularly, requiring IT professionals to keep their knowledge current. Taking online courses, earning certifications, attending conferences, and participating in webinars help maintain technical proficiency. Setting aside time for regular study and practice ensures that skills remain relevant and competitive in the job market.

Gaining hands-on experience is just as important as theoretical knowledge. Many IT professionals start with certifications or academic degrees, but real-world practice solidifies understanding. Setting up home labs, contributing to open-source projects, working on freelance assignments, or volunteering for IT-related tasks provide opportunities to apply skills in practical scenarios. Building a strong portfolio with real-world projects demonstrates expertise to potential employers and clients. Hands-on experience not only improves technical ability but also boosts confidence when solving complex IT problems.

Networking is a crucial factor in career growth. Many job opportunities come through personal connections rather than traditional applications. Attending industry meetups, joining IT-related online communities, and connecting with professionals on LinkedIn help expand a professional network. Engaging in discussions, sharing knowledge, and seeking mentorship open doors to career advancement. A strong network can provide guidance, job referrals, and insights into emerging trends in the industry. Maintaining professional relationships over time ensures access to valuable career opportunities.

Soft skills play a vital role in IT career success. While technical expertise is important, the ability to communicate effectively, work in teams, and solve problems efficiently makes a professional more valuable. Many IT jobs require collaboration between technical and non-technical teams, making clear communication essential. The ability to explain complex concepts in a simple manner helps build trust with colleagues, clients, and stakeholders. Developing skills in negotiation, leadership, and conflict resolution also prepares IT professionals for future managerial roles.

Time management and organization skills contribute to long-term success in IT. Many professionals work on multiple projects, requiring the ability to prioritize tasks efficiently. Learning how to break down complex problems, set realistic deadlines, and manage workloads reduces stress and improves productivity. Using project management tools, creating task lists, and setting clear goals help maintain focus. Developing strong organizational skills ensures that deadlines are met, projects are completed successfully, and clients or employers remain satisfied with performance.

Building a strong personal brand increases visibility and credibility in the IT industry. Professionals who share knowledge through blog posts, social media, open-source contributions, or speaking engagements establish themselves as experts in their field. Writing about IT topics, sharing insights on LinkedIn, or publishing tutorials on platforms like Medium or Dev.to demonstrates expertise. A well-maintained personal website or portfolio showcasing projects, certifications, and achievements creates a strong impression on recruiters and employers. Investing in a personal brand leads to greater recognition and career opportunities.

Understanding business needs and aligning IT skills with company goals makes professionals more valuable to employers. Many IT roles require not just technical expertise but also the ability to solve business problems effectively. Learning about industry-specific challenges, financial considerations, and customer needs enhances decision-making. IT professionals who understand how technology impacts business operations gain leadership opportunities. Those who develop skills in IT strategy, project management, and innovation contribute more significantly to organizational success.

Resilience and adaptability are essential for navigating challenges in an IT career. The industry is known for rapid change, unexpected technical issues, and high-pressure environments. Professionals who embrace challenges, learn from failures, and remain flexible will thrive in IT roles. Staying open to new technologies, adapting to industry shifts, and developing problem-solving skills ensure long-term career sustainability. The ability to remain calm under pressure and approach challenges with a positive attitude builds a strong professional reputation.

A willingness to mentor and help others strengthens both individual careers and the IT community as a whole. Many successful professionals attribute their growth to mentors who guided them early in their careers. Offering assistance to beginners, answering technical questions, or participating in mentorship programs fosters a culture of learning. Sharing knowledge benefits both mentors and mentees by reinforcing skills, building relationships, and creating opportunities for collaboration. The IT industry thrives on community-driven learning, making mentorship a valuable practice for professional growth.

Maintaining work-life balance is important for long-term career satisfaction. Many IT roles involve long hours, troubleshooting unexpected issues, or working on tight deadlines. Finding ways to manage stress, set boundaries, and take breaks improves productivity and prevents burnout. Engaging in hobbies, spending time with family, and maintaining a healthy lifestyle contribute to overall well-being. Professionals who take care of their mental and physical health perform better in their careers and maintain long-term motivation.

Preparing for career transitions ensures continued success in the IT field. As technology evolves, some roles become obsolete while new opportunities emerge. IT professionals who remain proactive in upskilling, exploring emerging fields, and staying adaptable are better positioned for career advancement. Whether moving into management, transitioning to a specialized technical role, or starting a business, planning for future career steps ensures steady progress. Regularly reassessing career goals and acquiring relevant skills keeps professionals ahead of industry trends.

The most successful IT professionals are those who remain curious, persistent, and passionate about learning. Developing expertise in a chosen field, staying connected with industry trends, and continuously improving skills create lasting career success. The IT industry rewards those who take initiative, embrace challenges, and strive for continuous growth. By following these strategies, professionals can build fulfilling and prosperous careers in the ever-evolving world of technology.

www.ingramcontent.com/pod-product-compliance
Lightning Source LLC
LaVergne TN
LVHW051233050326
832903LV00028B/2381